Lambda-Calculus, Combinators, and Functional Programming

Cambridge Tracts in Theoretical Computer Science

Titles in the Series

CAMBRIDGE UNIVERSITY PRESS
Cambridge, New York, Melbourne, Madrid, Cape Town, Singapore, São Paulo, Delhi

Cambridge University Press
The Edinburgh Building, Cambridge CB2 8RU, UK

Published in the United States of America by Cambridge University Press, New York

www.cambridge.org
Information on this title: www.cambridge.org/9780521114295

First published 1988
Reprinted 1989
This digitally printed version 2009

A catalogue record for this publication is available from the British Library

ISBN 978-0-521-34589-7 hardback
ISBN 978-0-521-11429-5 paperback

LAMBDA-CALCULUS, COMBINATORS, AND FUNCTIONAL PROGRAMMING

G. E. REVESZ

IBM Thomas J. Watson Research Center, Yorktown Heights, New York

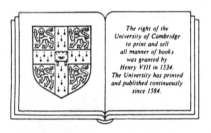

The right of the
University of Cambridge
to print and sell
all manner of books
was granted by
Henry VIII in 1534.
The University has printed
and published continuously
since 1584.

CAMBRIDGE UNIVERSITY PRESS

Cambridge

New York   Port Chester

Melbourne   Sydney

CONTENTS

PREFACE

There is a growing interest in lambda-calculus and combinators among computer scientists. The appeal of these abstract mathematical theories is due to their elementary yet quite universal nature. They seem to have successfully captured the most general formal properties of the notion of a mathematical function, which, in turn, is one of the most powerful concepts of modern mathematics.

The relevance of lambda-calculus to computer science is quite obvious in many cases. For instance, the design of the programming language LISP has been largely influenced by lambda-calculus. Also, the *call by name* mechanism of parameter correspondence used in ALGOL-like languages is closely related to the operation of formal substitution as defined precisely in lambda-calculus. The same is true for the textual substitution performed by macro generators. More recently John Backus and other proponents of functional style programming have strongly emphasized the importance of the function concept in computer science. Corresponding research efforts to develop efficient implementation techniques for functional languages have produced many interesting results in the theory of combinators as well as in lambda-calculus.

An explicit and systematic use of lambda-calculus in computer science was initiated by Peter Landin, Christopher Strachey, and a few others who started the development of a formal theory of semantics for programming languages based directly on lambda-calculus. Their approach is now called *denotational semantics* and it is widely accepted as a relevant theory. At first, however, denotational semantics was thought to be flawed by some experts, because of its naïve use of the type-free lambda-calculus, which did not seem to have any consistent mathematical model at that time. The first mathematical model for the type-free lambda-calculus was discovered by Dana Scott only in 1969 when he was trying to prove the nonexistence of such models. Since then, lambda-calculus and the theory of combinators have experienced a vigorous revival, which must have surprised even their originators, Alonso Church and Haskel B. Curry, who started their development in the early 30s.

Lambda-calculus may also play a more significant role in the theory of parallel algorithms in the future. It represents an abstract mathematical model of computation which is equivalent to the Turing machine. But, while the Turing machine is basically a sequential device, lambda-calculus can retain the implicit parallelism that is normally present in a mathematical expression. In pure mathematics, there is no such thing as the 'side effect' of a computation and thus, independent subexpressions may be computed in parallel. We can take advantage of this type of parallelism when using lambda-calculus.

This book approaches lambda-calculus and the theory of combinators from a computer scientist's point of view. It presents only their fundamental facts and some of their applications to functional programming in a self-contained manner. But, in contrast with the usual treatment of lambda-calculus in computer science texts, we present formal proofs for most of the results which are relevant to our discussion. At the same time, *lambda-calculus is treated here as a functional language implemented by software on a conventional computer.* It can also be implemented by hardware in a nonconventional computer whose machine code language would be lambda-calculus by itself. As a matter of fact, there already exist experimental machines whose instruction sets are fashioned after lambda-calculus and/or combinators.

As functional programming is coming of age, several more new hardware designs aimed at a direct execution of functional programs are likely to appear in the future. Some variant of lambda-calculus will certainly be used in most of them. Future generations of computers will probably have the speed and the necessary sophistication built in the hardware that may make them capable of running functional programs more efficiently, without placing the burden of controlling the parallelism on the programmer's shoulders.

As can be seen from the related literature, lambda-calculus represents the theoretical backbone of functional languages. Therefore, a systematic study of functional languages is hardly imaginable without a proper understanding of lambda-calculus, which is, in fact, the archetype of all functional or applicative languages. Many of the extra features of those languages can be treated in lambda-calculus as merely 'syntactic sugar'. A typical example is the composition of functions in Backus's FP system, or the ZF expressions (also called list comprehensions) in Miranda. Those features are, of course, very useful for the design of a practical functional language. The same is true for the various type systems which help program debugging at compile-time. The type-free lambda-calculus by itself is not a user oriented source language. It is rather a high-level machine oriented language, which is an ideal target language for the compilation of various functional languages.

The first three chapters of this book cover the fundamentals of type-free lambda-calculus. A special feature of the book is a new axiom system for beta-reduction presented in Section 2.5. This axiom system forms the basis of the graph-reduction technique discussed in Chapter 6, which is used for evaluating lambda-expressions. Another unique feature of the book is a direct extension of the lambda-notation to allow lists as primitive objects. This extension has been inspired by the so called 'construction', which is one of the combining forms in Backus's FP. An interesting fact about this combining form is that its defining property cannot be derived from the standard axioms of lambda-calculus. But, since it is independent of those axioms, we can add this property as a new axiom to the system. This way we obtain an extended lambda-calculus which is very convenient for list processing in a type-free manner.

The list-oriented features of our extended lambda-calculus are described in Chapter 4. These features allow for a very elegant treatment of mutual recursion. The discussion of semantics in Chapter 5 is based on the idea of program transformations using conversion rules. This leads to a formal definition of the semantics of the FP system designed by John Backus, since functional programs are easy to translate to the extended lambda-notation. Imperative programs are more difficult to translate, in general, unless they are 'well-structured'. This represents, by the way, an interesting justification for structured programming.

Many of the implementations proposed in the literature for functional languages make extensive use of lambda-calculus and/or combinators. In Chapter 6 of our book we describe a graph-reduction based interpreter for our extended lambda-calculus, which has been implemented on the IBM PC and then ported to some other IBM machines. A parallel version of the interpreter is currently being tested on a simulator of a shared memory multiprocessor machine. All the examples and the exercises included in this book have been checked out with the aid of the sequential interpreter, which can be used, by the way, as a software tool for a hands-on course on lambda-calculus. It can also be used for implementing other functional languages by translating them into our extended lambda-notation.

We hope that this book will help many computer scientists get acquainted with the basics of lambda-calculus and combinators, which, only a short while ago, were not fully appreciated by many mathematicians. The bibliographical notes at the end of the book are far from being complete. Nevertheless, they may serve as a starting point for a more thorough literature research in some selected areas by the reader.

The author gratefully acknowledges the support by the Thomas J. Watson Research Center of IBM, which provided the time and the tools, but most importantly the stimulating environment for writing this book.

CHAPTER ONE

INTRODUCTION

1.1 Variables and functions in mathematics and in programming languages

The use of variables in conventional programming languages is quite different from their use in mathematics. This has caused a great deal of difficulty in the definition of the meaning of a variable in programming languages like Fortran and Pascal. It is indeed very difficult to define exactly the meaning of a variable that is subject to various assignments within the scope of its declaration.

In a given mathematical context, every occurrence of a variable usually refers to the same value. Otherwise it would be impossible to talk about the solution of an equation like

$$x^2 = 2x + 3$$

For what can we say about the possible values of x, if we do not require that x represents the same value on each side of the equation?

This is in sharp contrast with the assignment statement in conventional programming languages. In Fortran, for example, one can write

    x = x + 1

knowing that the two occurrences of the variable x represent different values.

In mathematics we would use different variables or perhaps, different subscripts to distinguish the two values. Indeed, the assignment statement represents a new definition of the variable x, which must not be confused with its previous definition even if it has the same name.

The difference between the effect of an assignment statement and that of a new declaration of the same variable in a nested block (in a block-structured language) is quite substantial. The block structure clearly delineates the part of the program where the declaration is valid. This is called static scoping, since the scope of a declaration can be determined by the examination of the program text at compile time.

On the other hand, the scope, i.e. the lifetime of the definition of a variable established by an assignment statement will be terminated either by another assignment to the same variable or by leaving the block in which the variable is declared. Therefore, a mathematical description of the assignment statement is far from being trivial. One has to consider the *dynamic order*, i.e. the execution order of the statements in the program. But that may vary from one execution to the other depending on the input data. So, in fact, one has to consider all possible execution sequences to determine the scope of an assignment statement.

The assignment statement has no counterpart in standard mathematics. Still, the use of variables is not problem free. First of all, we have to distinguish between two entirely different ways of using variables in mathematical texts:

The first corresponds to the mental process of direct generalization. For example, we may think of an arbitrary natural number and denote it by the variable n, which is a direct generalization of the natural numbers, 1,2,3,... , by abstracting away from their particular values and considering only those properties which they have in common. With this, however, we maintain that n represents a fixed but otherwise arbitrary number throughout our discussion. It may, in fact, be implicitly defined by the equations and/or other relations we specify in our discussion. A variable used in this way is said to occur *free* in the given context.

Another way of using variables in mathematics is to let them run through a certain set of values. This is the case with the variable of integration in a formula like

$\int_0^1 e^x dx$

In this case the value of x is supposed to vary from 0 to 1 exhausting the set of all real numbers from the closed interval $[0,1]$. Another example is the use of the variable x in the following formula of predicate calculus:

$$\forall x[(x + 1)(x - 1) = x^2 - 1]$$

where the domain of x must be clear from the context. (Otherwise the domain should be explicitly stated in the formula itself.) Also, the existential quantifier in a formula like

$$\exists x(x^2 - 5x + 6 = 0),$$

expresses a property of the set of all possible values of x rather than a property shared by each of those values. A common feature of these formulas is the presence of some special symbol (integral, quantifier, etc.) which makes the formula meaningless, if the corresponding variable is replaced by a constant. (The formula $\forall 5[(5 + 1)(5 - 1) = 5^2 - 1]$ does not make much sense.) The variable in question is said to be *bound* in these formulas by the special symbol.

Now, the problem is that the distinction between the free and the bound usages of variables is not always obvious in every mathematical text. Quantifiers, for example, may be used implicitly or may be stated only verbally in the surrounding explanations. Also, a variable which is used as a free variable in some part of the text may be considered bound in a larger context.

The situation is even more confusing when we identify a function with its formula, without giving it any other name. If we say, for instance, that the function $x^3 - 3x^2 + 3x - 1$ is monotonic, or continuous, or its firts derivative is $3x^2 - 6x + 3$, then we consider the expression as a mapping and not as the representation of some value. So, the variable x is treated here as a bound variabe without explicitly being bound by some special symbol. As we shall see later, a major advantage of the lambda-notation is that it forces us to make the distinction between the free and the bound usages of variables always explicit. This is done by using a special binding symbol 'λ' for each of the bound variables occurring in an expression. Hence, we can specify a function by binding its argument(s), without giving it an extra name. The keyword 'lambda' is used for the same purpose in LISP. However, functions in programming languages are usually defined by function declarations where they must be given individual names.

Unfortunately, conventional programming languages treat function declarations and variable declarations in two different ways: *A function declaration is more like a constant definition than a variable declaration, because it explicitly assigns a given procedure to a function name.* Hence, we cannot have function type variables denoting arbitrary functions chosen from a given set. All we can do is to use arbitrary names for individually specified functions. To put it differently, functions are treated as second class citizens in most programming languages. They cannot occur on the left hand side of an assignment statement and cannot be returned as the result of a computation. Here we are talking about assignment statements of the form $f: = g$ where both f and g would be function names. This would amount to the assignment of the procedure itself used for the computation of g to the function name f. (This is not the same as using the function name to hold the value to be returned by the function for some given argument.) It is possible to pass a function name as a parameter to a procedure or function in Pascal, but function names can never be used as output variables or get their value in a read statement from a file. This clearly shows that they are treated differently from other variables.

There are no such restrictions in mathematics. Variables denoting functions are usually treated in the same manner as any other variables. They may, of course, have different domains, which is the subject of the next section. We must add, however, that the history of mathematics has also seen a substantial evolution of the function concept.

The original concept of a function was based on a computational procedure that would be used for computing its value for any given argument. This is the same as it is used today in most programming languages where each function is uniquely defined by a function procedure.

The development of the set theory, however, has replaced this procedural approach by a purely *extensional* view:

> *The set theoretical function definition postulates only the existence of a function value for any given argument without saying anything about the way of computing it.*

This view emphasizes the *extension* of a function as if it were completely given at once. This static, existential view of a function is in sharp contrast with its dynamic, procedural view.

*The procedural view presupposes the existence of a finite description
of the function in terms of a computing procedure.*

Here the set of values is not assumed to be immediately available, but it can
be produced dynamically by computing more and more elements from it.
This view is also called *intensional*, as opposed to the extensional view of
functions.

The relationship between these two different views of functions is far
from being trivial. It is obvious that different procedures may compute the
same *extensional* function. But, in general, it is undecidable whether two
procedurally defined functions are *extensionally equal*.

Definition 1.1 Two functions are *extensionally equal* if and only if
they have the same value for every argument. In symbols, $f = g$,
iff $f(x) = g(x)$ for all x.

Now, the problem of deciding the extensional equality of functions by ex-
amining their respective procedures is essentially the same as the equivalence problem of Turing machines, which is known to be unsolvable.

Nevertheless, there are various techniques for proving the equivalence
of certain procedures. The study of program transformations in computer
science is dealing with such techniques. Extensional equality is usually
called *semantic equality* or *semantic equivalence* in this context. This notion
is also relevant to program optimization, for the optimized program should
be semantically equivalent to the original one.

Naïve lambda-calculus can be thought of as an attempt at capturing
the most general formal properties of the extensional function concept using constructive, finitary methods. In this naïve sense, type-free lambda-
calculus was bound to encounter the same difficulties as naïve set theory.
The apparent paradoxes, after several unsuccessful attempts at avoiding
them, were thought to be inherent in the theory. The problem was put to
rest only in 1969, when Dana Scott showed that the intuitive interpretation
of the theory is reasonable if and only if it is restricted to the procedurally
definable (i.e., computable) functions.

As a purely constructive theory of procedurally well-defined functions,
type-free lambda-calculus is just as powerful as any other constructive approach. It is indeed equivalent to the theory of general recursive functions,
Turing machines, Markov algorithms, or any other constructive methods
for describing computational procedures in exact terms.

In this book type-free lambda-calculus is used in a purely constructive manner. Moreover, in Chapter 6 we shall describe an interpreter program for evaluating arbitrary lambda-exressions. This interpreter is implemented on the IBM PC and some other IBM machines.

1.2 Domains, types, and higher-order functions

According to the usual set-theoretical definition, every function has two fundamental sets associated with it namely, its *domain* and its *range* or *codomain*. Given these two sets, say D and R, a function is defined by a set of ordered pairs of the form

$$[[x,y] \mid x \in D, y \in R]$$

where the second component is uniquely determined by the first. Thus, for every x in D there is *at most one* y in R such that [x,y] belongs to a given function. If a function has *at least one*, hence, *exactly* one ordered pair [x,y] for every x ∈ D then it is called a *total* function on D; Otherwise it is called a *partial* function on D.

A function with domain D and range R is also called a mapping from D to R and its set of ordered pairs is called its *graph*. For nonempty D and R, there are, of course, many different functions from D to R, and each of them is said to be of type [D→R]. For finite D and R, the number of [D→R] type total functions is obviously $|R|^{|D|}$, where the name of a set between two vertical bars denotes the number of its elements. This formula extends to infinite sets with the cardinality of the given sets replacing the number of their elements. The set of all [D→R] type functions is also called the *function space* R^D.

If the range R has only two elements say, 0 and 1, then each [D→R] type total function is the characteristic function of a subset of D. Hence, the cardinality of the set of [D→R] type total functions with $|R| = 2$ is the same as that of the powerset of D. Therefore, if R has at least two elements, the cardinality of the function space R^D is larger than the cardinality of D.

So, for instance, the set of all number-theoretic, i.e. [N→N] type functions where N denotes the set of natural numbers, is clearly nondenumerable. On the other hand, it is known from the theory of algorithms that the set of computable functions is denumerable. Namely, each computable function must have a computational procedure, i.e. a Turing machine associated with it, and the set of all Turing machines can be enumerated in some sequence, say, according to the length of their descriptions encoded in some fixed alphabet. (Descriptions with the same length can be listed in lexicographic order.) This means that the overwhelming majority of the [N→N] type functions is noncomputable.

It is an interesting question if there is some extensionally definable property which would distinguish the graphs of computable functions from those of noncomputable ones. The mere fact that computable functions have Turing machines associated with them tells nothing directly about their properties as mappings. It would be nice if we could, so to speak, look at the graph of the function and tell if it is computable. Interestingly enough, there is such a property but it is far from being obvious. It is *'continuity'* in a somewhat unusual but interesting topology. Here, we do not discuss this topology but the interested reader is referred to the book by Joseph Stoy [Stoy77], or to the papers by Dana Scott [Scott73, Scott80]. For our discussion it suffices to say that the graphs of computable functions are indeed different from those of noncomputable ones, because they must obey certain restrictions namely, they must be 'continuous' in some abstract sense. The reason why we mention this continuity property is that it has been instrumental for the construction of a mathematical model for the type-free lambda-calculus.

The original purpose of type-free lambda-calculus was to provide a universal framework for studying the formal properties of arbitrary functions, which turned out to be a far too ambitious goal. Nevertheless, the type-free lambda-calculus can be used as a formal theory of functions in a wide variety of applications, but we should never try to apply this theory to noncontinuous, i.e. noncomputable functions. This state of the affairs is comparable to the development of set theory. Naïve set theory was meant to cover arbitrarily large sets. The paradoxical nature of that goal has led to the development of axiomatic set theory, where the notion of classes is introduced in order to avoid the paradoxes of arbitrarily large sets.

Now, as we know, the cardinality of the set of number-theoretic, i.e., $[N \rightarrow N]$ type functions is nondenumerable while the set of lambda-expressions is clearly denumerable, for it is a set of finite strings over a finite alphabet. Therefore, we cannot have a different lambda-expression for each number-theoretic function. But, if we restrict ourselves to 'continuous' functions then we can show that they are precisely those which can be described by lambda-expressions. This means that the set of 'continuous' functions coincides with the set of lambda-definable, hence, computable functions. In this book we are not concerned with this model-theoretic aspect of the theory but the interested reader is referred to the literature.

Typed lambda-calculus considers the domains and the ranges of functions as being relevant to their formal treatment. Function composition, for instance, is considered well-defined only for compatible types, i.e. when the range of the first function is the same as the domain of the second. In this theory each function has a unique type and, of course, there is an infinite variety of types. This approach is, in fact, a refinement of the type-free theory and it has a number of important applications. It serves as an appropriate model for strongly typed programming languages like Pascal or ADA.

In a strongly typed language every variable must have a type, which is basically the set of its possible values. This set, however, is usually endowed with some algebraic structure. So, for example, an **integer** type variable has two important characteristics:

(a) It can have only integer values
(b) It can be used as an argument only in those operations that are defined on integers.

The first requirement imposes a restriction on the effect of any assignment to that variable while the second requirement restricts its possible occurrences in the expressions.

A third aspect of a type is its relationship to other types, which is important for the discussion of possible (implicit or explicit) conversions between types.

Strongly typed languages usually have a finite set of *ground types* such as **integer, real, boolean,** or **character**, and any number of *user defined* or *constructed types* such as **arrays, records,** or *enumerated* types. Each ground type has a fixed set of primitive operations defined on it. These primitive operations have their own (implicit) types. The *test for zero* predicate for example, is of type $[\mathbf{N} \rightarrow \mathbf{B}]$, where $\mathbf{B} = \{\textbf{true}, \textbf{false}\}$.

New types can be defined by using certain *type constructors*. A **record** type, for instance, corresponds to the *cartesian product* of the types of its components. Thus, the domain of a record type variable is

$$D_1 \times D_2 \times \ldots \times D_n$$

where D_i is the domain of its i-th component.

Another type constructor is related to the so called 'variant records', which belong to the same file but have different structure. This construct corresponds to the set theoretical operation of *discriminated union*, denoted by

$$D_1 \oplus D_2 \oplus \ldots \oplus D_n$$

which is essentially the same as

$$D_1 \cup D_2 \cup \ldots \cup D_n$$

except that its elements will be discriminated (labelled) by their origins. This means that common elements will have as many copies as the number of the different D_i's to which they belong. So, for example, in a discriminated union of the types **integer** and **real** the integers will have two different (fixpoint vs. floating point) representations, which must be distinguished from one another.

The repeated application of the type constructors may result in fairly complex types, but this process is usually limited to the construction of *data types*. The construction of *function types*, i.e. function spaces is not supported by conventional languages.

The function space $\mathbf{R}^{\mathbf{D}}$ is also a set, so it can be used as the domain and/or the range of other functions. A mapping from $\mathbf{R}^{\mathbf{D}}$ to itself, which takes a function as an argument and returns another function as its value, is called a *functional* or *higher-order* function. The same construction can be repeated, which yields an infinite hierarchy of function spaces with ever increasing cardinalities. The corresponding functions can be classified according to this hierarchy and thus, we can talk about first order, second order, etc... functions relative to the given ground types.

The usefulness of an infinite hierarchy may be arguable, but certain functionals may be quite useful in many applications. Take for instance the symbolic differentiation of functions. It is clearly a second order function as it takes a function as an argument and returns another function as a result.

The implementation of function types seems more difficult than that of the ground types or other constructed types. The main difficulty, however, is due to the machine code representation of functions on conventional computers. It is namely much more difficult to manipulate the machine code representation of a function than to manipulate the machine representation of an integer or a real number. This has nothing to do with the cardinality of the function space, because we do not have to manipulate those infinite sets. All we have to do is to manipulate the finite representations of their elements just as we do with the integers or reals.

In the present state of the art, function manipulations are called *symbolic computations*, and they are treated differently from *numeric computations*. In lambda-calculus, as we shall see, the distinction between symbolic and numeric computations is irrelevant.

1.3 Polymorphic functions and Currying

Strong typing seems to be an uncomfortable straight jacket sometimes. A typical example is the problem of writing a generalized sort routine which should work the same way for integer, real, or character type keys. In a strongly typed language we cannot have variables with flexible types, so we actually need three versions of the sort routine, one for each type. Even if we have only, say, integer type keys, we cannot sort arbitrary records. By using variant records we can specify only a finite number of different record types, but we cannot have an open ended record type.

Similar problems occur in the context of list manipulation. There are functions, such as the length of a list, which are independent of the type of the elements in the list. Also, the usual operations on a push-down store, i.e. popping and pushing, are independent of the type of the elements stored in the stack.

A reasonable compromise between strong typing and a completely type free treatment of functions is represented by the use of *polymorphic functions.* Polymorphism in a typed language means using variables with flexible types. *A function is called polymorphic if the type of (at least one of) its arguments may vary from call to call.* Take, for example, the function *ADD* which is defined as the usual addition on integer type arguments while it is defined as the logical *OR* operation on Boolean type arguments. This is a polymorphic function, but, because of its rather arbitrary definition, it is an example of the so called *ad hoc* polymorphism.

A more interesting kind of polymorphism is one that is based on the structural similarities of certain domains. For example, the ordering of the integers under the usual $<$ relation is similar to the alphabetic ordering of character strings in an alphabet. We can take advantage of this similarity by using a polymorphic function for comparison which would take either integer or character type arguments. This way we can write 'generic' programs which implement the same algorithms for different types.

Typed λ-calculus can be extended to polymorphic types, which makes it more attractive as a formal theory of types for modern programming languages. An excellent discussion of the various kinds of polymorphism can be found in [Ca-W85], which also contains a good overview of the evolution of types in programming languages. A brief introduction to typed λ-calculus will be given as Appendix B at the end of this book.

One of the main concerns of type theory is the question of type equivalence, which is clearly related to the problem of type checking. The whole point of type checking is to establish the equality (or at least the compatibility) of the types of certain variables occurring in a program. This is far from being a trivial task except for very simple cases. The ground types and the type constructors represent, in fact, an algebra of types, where certain types may be constructed in many different ways. If, for example, we combine three records simply by concatenating them then the resulting record type corresponds to $D_1 \times D_2 \times D_3$ where D_i is the domain of the i-th record. Notice the fact that no parentheses are used here, because the Cartesian product is associative. In other words, we get the same record type if we concatenate the first two records and then concatenate the resulting record and the third one, or the other way around.

In general, however, it is very difficult to decide whether or not two different type constructions result in the same domain. Type checking is, therefore, a major problem for programming languages with nontrivial type systems. Some of the difficulties may be avoided by treating the type

specifications as purely formal expressions rather than representations of
sets. Different type specifications may then be considered different even
if the corresponding domains are actually the same. For a practical system,
however, we have to allow at least some obvious equalities between different type specifications. (For instance, a file type with variant records
should not be sensitive to the order of enumerating the variants.) The
complexity of the type specifications may increase substantially, if we allow recursively defined types. The use of polymorphic types does not make
type checking much simpler.

The type of a function is clearly related to its 'arity', which is the
number of its arguments. Indeed, the domain of a binary function is the
Cartesian product of the respective domains of its two arguments. So, for
instance, the addition of integers is of type $[N \times N \rightarrow N]$.

Addition and multiplication are usually extended to any finite number
of arguments. *A function which can take an arbitray number of arguments
is called polyadic.* Thus, the domain of a polyadic function is the union of
the corresponding cartesian products. For example, the domain of the integer Σ function is

$$N \cup (N \times N) \cup (N \times N \times N) \cup \ldots$$

Conventional programming languages do not allow polyadic functions.
The number of formal parameters specified in a function declaration will
determine the number of arguments that *must* be supplied in each call of
the given function.

To overcome this limitation one can use sequences (i.e., arrays or lists)
as arguments. *Using lists as arguments is quite common in functional languages.* It seems that a uniform treatment of functions can be achieved by
using only unary functions which take only lists as arguments. This way
we can have polyadic functions in disguise, but there is a price to pay.
Namely, many practical functions make sense only with a fixed number of
arguments. The implementation of such functions must check the length
of the argument list before using it.

This approach was taken by John Backus in the design of the functional language FP, where the usual arithmetic operations are treated as
unary functions with ordered pairs as arguments [Back78]. The type of the
argument, however, is specified as a list, which may have any number of

elements. Therefore, it is the responsibility of the implementation to make sure that the argument has precisely two elements.

Another method of representing all functions by unary ones is called **Currying**, after Haskell B. Curry. This method was introduced by Schönfinkel [Schö24] and extensively used by Curry. It consists of transforming multi-argument functions into sequences of unary functions. Let us take again addition for an example. The + function takes two arguments, so it is of type

$$[N \times N \to N].$$

But, if we supply only one argument then we get a unary function which would add a constant (the given operand) to its only argument (the missing operand). The resulting functions can be denoted by

add1, add2, add3, ...

and they are clearly of type $[N \to N]$. So, that is the range of the first function, which is, therefore, of type

$$[N \to [N \to N]]$$

Hence, the process of Currying of a function can be described informally as exchanging each × symbol in its domain for an → in its range. The Curry-ed version of an n-argument function on integers will have the type

$$[N \to ... [N \to [N \to N]]...]$$

where precisely *n* arrows occur. For that, of course, we need higher order, or at least function valued functions which are not readily available in conventional programming languages. But, in the type-free lambda-calculus, where functions of any type are treated in the same way, Currying represents a useful device for replacing multi-argument functions by repeated applications of unary ones. As we mentioned before, the implementation of higher order functions is not as difficult as it might appear at first.

CHAPTER TWO

TYPE-FREE LAMBDA-CALCULUS

2.1 Syntactic and semantic considerations

As we have mentioned in the introduction, the purpose of the lambda-calculus is to study the most general properties of functions. This means that we want to develop a unified theory of functions encompassing all kinds of functions used in various parts of mathematics. One way of doing this is to use set theory as a foundation and build the notion of a function on the notion of a set. This is the usual approach taken by modern mathematics, which corresponds to the extensional view of functions. According to this notion, a function is just a (usually infinite) set of ordered pairs where the first member of each pair is an argument value while the second member is the corresponding value of the function. This approach has important theoretical benefits as manifested by the development of modern mathematics, but it is clearly a departure from the original formula-based function concept.

In lambda-calculus functions are represented by symbolic notations called λ-expressions and not by sets of ordered pairs. These λ-expressions can be manipulated directly and thus, we can build a theory of function transformations using this symbolic representation of functions. The question is what kinds of functions are represented by these λ-expressions, and what kinds of operations can be performed on them by manipulating their representations? Strangely enough, the first question is much more difficult to answer than the second. In fact, we shall define the syntax of λ-expressions without defining their semantics right away. Next, we shall define certain operations on λ-expressions and investigate their properties under these operations. This way we will study a purely formal system hoping that these symbolic expressions are indeed representations of existing functions. A justification for this naïve approach will be given later in Chapter 5 where the related semantic issues will be discussed.

For the time being, we shall assume that every λ-expression denotes some function. Moreover, we shall consider arbitrary functions regardless of their types. This means that we will not be concerned with the domain and the range of a function, since we are interested only in those properties which are common to all functions. Now, the question is whether such properties exist, and, if so, whether they are interesting enough for developing a meaningful theory about them. The rest of this book should provide a positive answer to both of these questions. It is concerned namely, with the development of the type-free lambda-calculus which, in fact, represents a general framework also for its typed versions.

The type-free theory is obviously more general, but its relevance had been strongly debated for quite some time until it gained universal acceptance by the end of the sixties. Today it is widely used in theoretical computer science and even for such practical purposes as the hardware design of non-conventional computer architectures. As we shall see later in this book, lambda-calculus is one of the most important tools for studying the mathematical properties of programming languages. Historically, it has been developed for similar purposes regarding the language of mathematical logic, but it has been greatly rejuvenated by the latest developments in computer science. Now, let us see the formal definition of λ-expressions.

First, we assume that there is an infinite sequence of *variables* and a finite or infinite sequence of *constants*. Each variable will be represented by an identifier (i.e., by a finite string of symbols chosen from some finite alphabet) as is usual in programming languages like Pascal or LISP. Similarly, each constant will be represented by a finite string of digits and/or symbols chosen from a finite set of available symbols.

Variables and constants are called *atoms* since they are the simplest λ-expressions. More complex λ-expressions can be built from them by using two expression forming operations, application and abstraction.

An *application* is simply the application of one λ-expression to another. The first of these two λ-expressions is called the *operator*, the second is called the *operand* in that application. This means that any λ-expression can be used both as an operator and as an operand with no restriction at all. (Note that we are not concerned with the meaning of such applications at the present time.)

An *abstraction* is formed with the special symbol λ followed by a variable, followed by a dot, followed by an arbitrary λ-expression. The purpose of the operation of abstraction is to make a unary function from a given λ-expression. The variable occurring next to the leading λ gives the name of the argument. Functions with more than one argument are formed by repeated abstractions. A formal definition of λ-expressions is given by the following syntax:

THE SYNTAX OF LAMBDA-EXPRESSIONS

<λ-expression>::=<variable>|<constant>|<application>|<abstraction>

<application>::=(<λ-expression>)<λ-expression>

<abstraction>::=λ<variable>.<λ-expression>

This syntax allows us to form λ-expressions like

    λx.x   λx.λy.(y)x

    λx.(f)x   (f)3

    λf.(f)2   (λy.(x)y)λx.(u)x

whose meanings are left undefined for the time being. Nevertheless, we will treat them as functional expressions which satisfy certain formal requirements.

A remark on our nonconventional way of parenthesizing lambda-expressions may be in order here. The traditional way of putting the argument(s) of a function between parentheses may have been suggested by the conventional way of evaluating a function. In the conventional or applicative order of evaluation, the argument of a function is computed before the application. That corresponds to the *call by value* mechanism of parameter passing in programming languages. In this book we use the notation (f)x instead of the traditional f(x), which reflects the so called normal order or left-to-right evaluation strategy, where the function itself is analyzed first before looking at the argument.

Our syntax represents an LL(1) grammar for lambda-expressions, which is very useful for the development of an efficient predictive parser. (Every application starts with a left parenthesis, and every abstraction starts with a λ.) Every left parenthesis can thus be treated as a *prefix* '*apply operator*' with the corresponding right parenthesis being just a delimiter. The main reason, however, for using this notation is its simplicity. The traditional notation often requires the use of parentheses both in the function and in the argument part of a lambda-expression. That may become quite confusing when dealing with complicated lambda-expressions. LISP has already departed from the traditional notation by using (f x) instead. Here we go one step further by using (f)x, which seems more natural and easier to follow when working with *Curried* functions.

The syntactic structure of a λ-expression is defined by its parse tree with respect to the above context-free grammar. This grammar is unambiguous, hence, every λ-expression has a unique parse tree. The subtrees of this parse tree correspond to the subexpressions of the given λ-expression. The same subexpression may have, of course, several occurrences in a larger expression.

In this book we shall use small letters, x, y, z, etc., as generic names for arbitrary variables. Arbitrary λ-expressions will usually be denoted by capital letters, P, Q, R, etc..

*Two λ-expressions, P and Q, are **identical**, in symbols P ≡ Q, if and only if Q is an exact (symbol by symbol) copy of P.*

As can be seen from our syntax, functional application associates to the right. The λ-expression (P)(Q)R is namely, the application of P to (Q)R, while the λ-expression ((P)Q)R denotes the application of (P)Q to R.

An occurrence of a variable x in a λ-expression E is said to be **bound** if it is inside a subterm with the form λx.P; otherwise it is *free*.

Definition 2.1. The set of the free variables of a λ-expression E, denoted by $\phi(E)$, is defined by induction on the construction of E as follows:

(1) $\phi(c) = \{\}$ (i.e., the empty set) if c is a constant

(2) $\phi(x) = \{x\}$ for any variable x

(3) $\phi(\lambda x.P) = \phi(P) - \{x\}$

(4) $\phi((P)Q) = \phi(P) \cup \phi(Q)$

Note that the same variable may occur both free and bound in a λ-expression. For instance, the first occurrence of x in

$(\lambda x.(z)x)\lambda y.(y)x$

(apart from its occurrence in the λx prefix) is bound, while its second occurrence is free. Thus, the set of free variables in this example is {x, z}, but not every occurrence of x is free.

The two occurrences of y in the following λ-expression

$\lambda y.(\lambda x.(x)y)\lambda y.(y)x$

are bound by two separate λy prefixes. Each λy represents an abstraction with respect to y, but it affects only those occurrences of y which are free in the subexpression prefixed by the given λy. More details on the usage of the abstraction can be found in the next Section.

Constants may be treated as special variables which can never be used as bound variables. They represent fairly trivial special cases in most definitions and theorems. *For the sake of simplicity, constants will be omitted from the definitions and the proofs that follow in this chapter and in Appendix A.*

2.2 Renaming, α-congruence, and substitution

The computation of the value of a function for some argument requires the substitution of the argument for the corresponding variable in the expression representing the function. This is a fundamental operation in mathematics as well as in programming languages. In a programming language like Pascal or Fortran, this corresponds to the substitution of the actual parameters for the so called formal parameters. In lambda-calculus both the function and the arguments are represented by λ-expressions, and every function is written as a unary function which may return another function as its value. So, for instance, the operation of addition will be represented here as

$\lambda x.\lambda y.((+)x)y.$

A fundamental aspect of the use of bound variables is expressed by the following:

Two lambda-expressions are considered essentially the same if they differ only in the names of their bound variables.

For instance, the λ-expressions $\lambda x.(y)x$ and $\lambda z.(y)z$, represent the same function, because the choice of the name of the bound variable has no influence on the meaning of a function. The same is true for programming languages where the formal parameters occurring in a function declaration are only dummies, i.e. place holders for the actual arguments, so we can choose arbitrary names for them. This freedom of choice is formalized in lambda-calculus via a transformation called α-conversion. It is just a renaming of bound variables which would not change the meaning of λ-expressions.

Definition 2.2. The **renaming** of a variable x to z in a λ-expression P, in symbols $\{z/x\}P$, is defined by induction on the construction of P as follows:

(1) $\{z/x\}x \equiv z$

(2) $\{z/x\}y \equiv y$ if $x \not\equiv y$

(3) $\{z/x\}\lambda x.E \equiv \lambda z.\{z/x\}E$ for every λ-expression E.

(4) $\{z/x\}\lambda y.E \equiv \lambda y.\{z/x\}E$ for every λ-expression E, if $x \not\equiv y$

(5) $\{z/x\}(E_1)E_2 \equiv (\{z/x\}E_1)\{z/x\}E_2$ for any two λ-expressions, E_1 and E_2.

Note that the renaming prefix $\{z/x\}$ is not a proper part of the λ-notation, as it is not included in the syntax of λ-expressions. The notation $\{z/x\}P$ is just a shorthand for the λ-expression obtained from P by performing the prescribed renaming. For example, the notation

$\{a/b\}(\lambda v.\lambda b.(b)v)\lambda u.((c)u)b$

stands for the λ-expression

$(\lambda v.\lambda a.(a)v)\lambda u.((c)u)a$

as can be easily verified by the reader.

Definition 2.2 will never be applied with $z \equiv x$ or $z \equiv y$, because renaming will be used only for α-*conversion* as described by the following rule:

THE ALPHA-RULE

(α) $\lambda x.E \rightarrow_a \lambda z.\{z/x\}E$ for any z which is neither free nor bound in E.

We say that the λ-expression on the left-hand side is α-*convertible* to the one on the right-hand side. Since x is neither free nor bound in $\{z/x\}E$, the reverse of a renaming is also a renaming. Hence, α-convertibility is a symmetric relation. Clearly, it is also transitive. Next we define α-*congruence or α-equality*.

> **Definition 2.3.** Two λ-expressions, M and N, are α-**congruent** (or α-**equal**), in symbols $M \cong N$, if either $M \equiv N$, or $M \rightarrow_a N$, or N is obtained from M by replacing a subexpression S of M by a λ-expression T such that $S \rightarrow_a T$, or there is some λ-expression R such that $M \cong R$ and $R \cong N$.

The notion of α-congruence is clearly an equivalence (reflexive, symmetric, and transitive) relation. It will be generalized shortly to permit more interesting 'meaning preserving' transformations on λ-expressions. We are now prepared for giving a precise formal definition of the operation of substitution.

> **Definition 2.4.** The **substitution** of Q for all free occurrences of the variable x in P, in symbols $[Q/x]P$, is defined inductively as follows:
>
> (1) $[Q/x]x \cong Q$
>
> (2) $[Q/x]y \cong y$ if $x \not\equiv y$.
>
> (3) $[Q/x]\lambda x.E \cong \lambda x.E$ for any λ-expression E.
>
> (4) $[Q/x]\lambda y.E \cong \lambda y.[Q/x]E$ for any λ-expression E, if $x \not\equiv y$ and at least one of these two conditions holds: $x \notin \phi(E)$, $y \notin \phi(Q)$.
>
> (5) $[Q/x]\lambda y.E \cong \lambda z.[Q/x]\{z/y\}E$ for any λ-expression E and for any z with $x \not\equiv z \not\equiv y$ which is neither free nor bound in $(E)Q$, if $x \not\equiv y$ and both $x \in \phi(E)$ and $y \in \phi(Q)$ hold.
>
> (6) $[Q/x](E_1)E_2 \cong ([Q/x]E_1)[Q/x]E_2$

Again, the substitution prefix [Q/x] is not part of the λ-notation, as it is not included in our syntax. The notation [Q/x]P is just an abbreviation for the λ-expression obtained from P by carrying out the prescribed substitution.

Example: The substitution

[λz.λy.(y)z/x](λu.(x)u)(u)x

is defined as being α-congruent to

([λz.λy.(y)z/x]λu.(x)u)[λz.λy.(y)z/x](u)x

that is

(λu.[λz.λy.(y)z/x](x)u)([λz.λy.(y)z/x]u)[λz.λy.(y)z/x]x

that is

(λu.([λz.λy.(y)z/x]x)[λz.λy.(y)z/x]u)(u)λz.λy.(y)z

and finally

(λu.(λz.λy.(y)z)u)(u)λz.λy.(y)z

which is already a proper λ-expression.

This example shows that the substitution operation may get quite complex when we are working with complicated λ-expressions. The most intriguing case is covered by part (5) of Definition 2.4 where we have to introduce a new bound variable z in order to avoid the capture of the free occurrence(s) of y in Q. If we did not have this clause and wanted to use (4) instead naïvely, i.e. without any restrictions, then we would get some errors as can be seen from the following example:

[λu.(y)u/x]λy.(x)y

would yield

λy.[λu.(y)u/x](x)y

and then

λy.([λu.(y)u/x]x)[λu.(y)u/x]y

and finally

λy.(λu.(y)u)y

This means that the free occurrence of y in λu.(y)u would become bound in the result, which is clearly against our intuition about substitution. Indeed, the free occurrence of y in the substitution prefix should not be confused with the bound variable y in the target expression. In order to avoid this confusion we introduce a new bound variable z which gives the correct result namely,

$$\lambda z.(\lambda u.(y)u)z$$

It should be noted in this regard that *the result of a substitution* is not a unique λ-expression, since it *is defined only up to α-congruence*. But it is easy to see that

$$\lambda z.[Q/x]\{z/y\}E \cong \lambda v.[Q/x]\{v/y\}E$$

if both z and v satisfy the condition of part (5) of Definition 2.4. (See Exercise 2.3 at the end of Chapter 2.) This is quite satisfactory for our purpose, because we are not so much interested in the identity of λ-expressions as in their equality.

This freedom of choice with respect to the new bound variables while performing a substitution has been achieved by our simplified renaming operation which is defined directly without using substitution.

Our approach is slightly different from the conventional definition of substitution included in most textbooks where every effort is made to define a unique result for the substitution operation. We feel, however, that the conventional approach imposes a rather artificial and unnecessary restriction on the choice of the bound variable used for renaming during substitution. Its only gain is that renaming becomes a special case of substitution and thus, it can be denoted by [z/x].

The complications with the substitution operation have inspired some researchers to try to get rid of bound variables altogether. This has resulted in the discovery of combinators which we shall study in Chapter 3. For the time being, we can be satisfied that Definition 2.4 is a precise formal definition of the substitution operation in the type-free lambda-calculus.

2.3 Beta-reduction and equality

The substitution operation defined in the previous section is one of the most important operations in classical λ-calculus. It allows the simplification of certain λ-expressions without changing their meanings. This is expressed by the following rule:

THE BETA-RULE

(β) $(\lambda x.P)Q \rightarrow [Q/x]P$

For arbitrary x, P, and Q, the λ-expression $(\lambda x.P)Q$ is called a β-redex while the corresponding right-hand side is called its *contractum*. Remember that the λ-expression on the right-hand side is defined only up to α-congruence.

   The contractum of a β-redex is usually simpler than the β-redex itself. For instance, the contractum of $(\lambda x.x)Q$ is Q while the contractum of $(\lambda x.y)Q$ is y. In both cases the resulting λ-expressions have fewer applications and fewer abstractions than the original ones. But that is not always true as can be seen from this example:

   $(\lambda x.(x)x)\lambda x.(x)x \rightarrow [\lambda x.(x)x/x]\lambda x.(x)x \cong (\lambda x.(x)x)\lambda x.(x)x$

The contractum of this β-redex is α-congruent with itself, although β-contraction in general is neither reflexive nor symmetric. It can be used, however, to define an equivalence relation on λ-expressions which is called β-equality or simply *equality*. First we define β-reduction.

   Definition 2.5. The relation $M \Rightarrow N$ (read M β-*reduces* to N) is defined inductively as follows:

   (1) $M \Rightarrow N$ if $M \cong N$.

   (2) $M \Rightarrow N$ if $M \rightarrow N$ is an instance of the β-rule.

   (3) If $M \Rightarrow N$ for some M and N, then for any λ-expression E, both $(M)E \Rightarrow (N)E$ and $(E)M \Rightarrow (E)N$ also hold.

   (4) If $M \Rightarrow N$ for some M and N then for any variable x, $\lambda x.M \Rightarrow \lambda x.N$ also holds.

   (5) If $M \Rightarrow E$ and $E \Rightarrow N$ then also $M \Rightarrow N$.

---

(6)   M $\Rightarrow$ N only in those cases as specified by (1) through (5).

This means that M β-reduces to N if N is obtained from M by replacing a part of M of the form $(\lambda x.P)Q$ by its contractum $[Q/x]P$, or N is obtained from M by a finite (perhaps empty) sequence of such replacements. The relation $\Rightarrow$ is clearly reflexive and transitive but not symmetric. It is defined on the α-equivalence classes of λ-expressions rather than on the λ-expressions themselves. In other words, M $\Rightarrow$ N is invariant under α-conversion. Now we can extend the notion of α-equality by forming the symmetric and transitive closure of $\Rightarrow$.

> **Definition 2.6.** M is β-*convertible* (or simply *equal*) to N, in symbols M = N, iff M $\cong$ N, or M $\Rightarrow$ N, or N $\Rightarrow$ M, or there is a λ-expression E such that M = E and E = N.

This notion of equality is defined in a purely formal manner with no reference to the 'meaning' at all. Nevertheless, it is relevant to the meaning, because it says that the meaning of λ-expressions must be invariant under β-conversion. This is, in a sense, a minimum requirement regarding all possible definitions of the meaning.

Now the question arises, how to decide whether two λ-expressions are equal or not. Unfortunately, this question in general is algorithmically undecidable. Note that we are not talking about a more elaborate notion of semantic equivalence. All we are talking about is β-convertibility. This may be disappointing but we can look at it this way: As we have said, β-*convertibility* represents a special case of the *extensional* equality. Since it is already undecidable, then it might, in fact, be equivalent to it. As a matter of fact, β-conversion turns out to be 'almost' equivalent to extensional equality. It represents a very useful and general tool for comparing various functions. (See also Lemma 3.1 and the η-rule in Section 3.4.)

The process of β-reduction is aimed at the simplification of λ-expressions. It terminates when no more β-redexes remain in the given λ-expression. This gives rise to the notion of the *normal form* of lambda-expressions.

> A λ-*expression is said to be in **normal form** if no β-redex, i.e. no subexpression of the form $(\lambda x.P)Q$ occurs in it.*

Such a λ-expression cannot be reduced any further so, in this sense, it is the simplest among all those λ-expressions which are equal to it. But, there exist λ-expressions like

$(\lambda x.(x)x)\lambda x.(x)x$

for which β-reduction never terminates. This is the main reason for the undecidability of the equality of arbitrary λ-expressions.

It should be emphasized that for certain λ-expressions there are terminating as well as nonterminating β-reductions. But, *if there is at least one terminating β-reduction then we say that the given λ-expression has a normal form.* For instance, the normal form of the λ-expression

$(\lambda y.(\lambda z.w)y)(\lambda x.(x)x)\lambda x.(x)x$

happens to be

w

in spite of the fact that it also has a nonterminating β-reduction as we have seen before.

Fortunately, if a λ-expression has at least one terminating β-reduction, then one can find such a β-reduction in a straightforward manner without 'back-tracking'. This follows from the so called standardization theorem to be discussed later in Chapter 6. Moreover, if a λ-expression has a normal form then every terminating β-reduction would result in the same normal form (up to α-congruence).

In other words, the order in which the β-redexes are contracted is irrelevant as long as the reduction terminates. This is a corollary of the Church–Rosser theorem, which is one of the most important results of the theory of lambda-conversion. As we shall see below, this theorem also implies that the equality problem of λ-expressions having normal forms is decidable.

2.4 The Church–Rosser theorem

The validity of the Church–Rosser theorem seems quite natural in view of our experience with elementary algebra. Its proof, however, is surprisingly difficult. Fortunately, the theorem itself is easy to understand without working through the proof. Therefore, we do not discuss the proof here, but it can be found in Appendix A at the end of this book. The essence of the theorem can be illustrated by the following example.

Assume that we have a polynomial P with two variables, x and y. In order to compute its value, say, for x = 3 and y = 4, we have to substitute 3 for x and 4 for y in P and perform the prescribed arithmetic operations. If we substitute only one of these values for the corresponding variable in P then we get a polynomial in the other variable. Now, either of these 'partially substituted' polynomials can be used to compute the value of the original polynomial for the given arguments by substituting the value of the remaining variable. In other words, the final result *does not depend on the order in which the substitutions are performed.*

If substitution is defined correctly, then this must be true in general. Indeed, for any λ-expressions, P, Q, and R, and variables, x and y, we have

$$(\lambda x.(\lambda y.P)R)Q \Rightarrow [Q/x](\lambda y.P)R \cong ([Q/x]\lambda y.P)[Q/x]R$$

$$\cong (\lambda z.[Q/x]\{z/y\}P)[Q/x]R \Rightarrow [[Q/x]R/z][Q/x]\{z/y\}P$$

At the same time we have

$$((\lambda x.(\lambda y.P)R)Q \Rightarrow (\lambda x.[R/y]P)Q \Rightarrow [Q/x][R/y]P$$

which, according to the Church–Rosser theorem, must be equal to the above.

Theorem 2.1 (Church–Rosser theorem I) If E ⇒ M and E ⇒ N then there is some Z such that M ⇒ Z and N ⇒ Z.

This theorem is represented by the diagram in Figure 2.1.

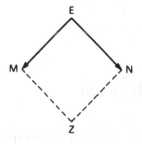

Figure 2.1

The property reflected by this diagram is called the *diamond property* (or *confluence property*). The Church-Rosser theorem says, in effect, that β-reduction has the diamond property.

> **Corollary:** If E ⇒ M and E ⇒ N, where both M and N are in normal form then M ≅ N.

In other words, every λ-expression has a *unique normal form* (up to α-congruence) provided that it has a normal form at all. This corollary follows immediately from the theorem, because, in this case, the existence of some Z with M ⇒ Z and N ⇒ Z implies that M ≅ Z ≅ N.

Now, for the question of β-equality the diamond property can be generalized this way:

> **Theorem 2.2** (Church–Rosser theorem II) If M = N then there is a Z such that M ⇒ Z and N ⇒ Z.

This second form of the Church–Rosser theorem follows from the diamond property by induction on the number of reductions and reverse reductions connecting M and N. Namely, by the definition of equality, M = N implies that there is a finite sequence of λ-expressions $E_0, E_1, ..., E_n$ such that $M \cong E_0$, $N \cong E_n$ and for every i $(0 \leq i < n)$ either $E_i \Rightarrow E_{i+1}$ or $E_{i+1} \Rightarrow E_i$. The proof is represented by the diagram in Figure 2.2, which shows the induction step using the diamond property.

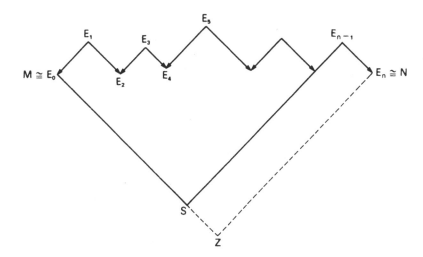

Figure 2.2

An immediate consequence of this second form of the Church–Rosser theorem is the following:

Corollary A: If N is in normal form and M = N then M ⇒ N.

Proof: According to the second Church–Rosser theorem there exists some λ-expression Z such that M ⇒ Z and N ⇒ Z. But, since N is in normal form, N ≅ Z must be the case and thus, M ⇒ N.

Further, if both M and N are in normal form then M = N implies M ≅ N, that is, *two equal expressions in normal form must be α-congruent.*

Here, we should add that for any two λ-expressions, M and N, *it is always decidable whether or not* M ≅ N. All we have to do is to rename systematically the bound variables in each λ-expression so that the name of a bound variable will be determined uniquely by the order in which the binding λ's occur. This way the decision of α-equality can be reduced to an identity check, which is trivial. Finally, we state the following:

Corollary B: If M = N, then either M and N both have the same normal form (up to α-congruence) or else neither of them has a normal form.

Again, this follows immediately from the Church–Rosser theorem. So, the question of the equality of λ-expressons can be reduced to the problem of deciding whether or not they have normal forms. But, unfortunately, that is in general undecidable. It is, of course, possible to show that certain λ-expressions are equal (i.e. β-convertible) in spite of the fact that they have no normal form. The problem is that in general we cannot determine in a finite number of steps whether or not they are equal when they have no normal form.

2.5 Beta-reduction revisited

As we mentioned before, the substitution operator is not as simple as may be desirable for many applications. The substitution prefix is not a proper part of the lambda-notation, and each time it appears during β-reduction, it should be eliminated by using its recursive definition. The number of it-eration steps required for the elimination of the substitution prefix depends on the construction of the λ-expression in question. This cannot be considered an elementary operation, so it is reasonable to look for an alternative definition of β-reduction which would be based on more elementary operations. This can be achieved simply by decomposing the substitution operation into more elementary steps.

This means that we can define β-reduction by making essential use of the properties of the substitution operation without explicitly referring to it. This way we get five different β-rules, instead of the original one, but the new β-rules do not involve any recursion. Moreover, we can do away completely with the substitution prefix and stay within the limits of the pure lambda-notation. Even the renaming operation becomes superfluous, if we adopt the following α-rule:

THE REVISED ALPHA-RULE

(α) $\lambda x.E \rightarrow \lambda z.(\lambda x.E)z$ for any $z \notin \phi(E)$

Note that this new α-rule is not symmetric by definition and it would not perform any renaming by itself. But the following β-rules would take care of the renaming, as well.

THE REVISED BETA-RULES

$(\beta 1)$ $(\lambda x.x)Q \rightarrow Q$

$(\beta 2)$ $(\lambda x.y)Q \rightarrow y$ if x and y are different variables.

$(\beta 3)$ $(\lambda x.\lambda x.E)Q \rightarrow \lambda x.E$

$(\beta 4)$ $(\lambda x.\lambda y.E)Q \rightarrow \lambda y.(\lambda x.E)Q$ if x and y are different variables, and
          at least one of these two conditions holds: $x \notin \phi(E)$, $y \notin \phi(Q)$.

$(\beta 5)$ $(\lambda x.(E_1)E_2)Q \rightarrow ((\lambda x.E_1)Q)(\lambda x.E_2)Q$

A λ-expression with the form $\lambda x.E$ is called an α-redex without any restriction. However, a term of the form $(\lambda x.E)Q$ is a β-redex if and only if it has the form of the left-hand side of a β-rule and satisfies its conditions. In particular, a λ-expression of the form $(\lambda x.\lambda y.E)Q$ with different x and y and with $x \in \phi(E)$ and $y \in \phi(Q)$ is not a β-redex. Such a λ-expression can be reduced only after an appropriate renaming is carried out. This can be initiated by an α-reduction of $\lambda y.E$ which yields $(\lambda x.\lambda z.(\lambda y.E)z)Q$ with $z \notin \phi(Q)$.

It should be noted that the contractum of a β-redex is uniquely defined in this system, since for every β-redex there is at most one β-rule that is applicable to it. In order to see how this system works we prove a few basic lemmas. But first of all, we have to redefine the notions of β-reduction and equality.

Definition 2.7 The relation $M \Rightarrow N$ (read M *reduces* to N) is defined as follows:

(1) $M \Rightarrow N$ if $M \equiv N$.

(2) $M \Rightarrow N$ if $M \rightarrow N$ is an instance of the new α-rule or one of the β-rules.

(3)   If $M \Rightarrow N$ for some λ-expressions, M and N, then both $(M)E \Rightarrow (N)E$ and $(E)M \Rightarrow (E)N$ for any λ-expression E.

(4)   If $M \Rightarrow N$ for some λ-expressions, M and N, then $\lambda x.M \Rightarrow \lambda x.N$ for any variable x.

(5)   If there is a λ-expression E such that $M \Rightarrow E$ and $E \Rightarrow N$ then $M \Rightarrow N$.

(6) $M \Rightarrow N$ only in those cases as specified by (1) through (5).

According to this definition *reduction* is reflexive and transitive. Equality can be defined again as the symmetric and transitive closure of $\Rightarrow$.

Definition 2.8 M is *convertible* (or simply *equal*) to N, in symbols $M = N$, iff $M \equiv N$ or $M \Rightarrow N$ or $N \Rightarrow M$ or there is a λ-expression E such that $M = E$ and $E = N$.

Now, we can prove that this new definition of equality is equivalent to the original one. First we prove some basic facts.

Lemma 2.1 If $M \Rightarrow N$ and $x \in \phi(N)$ then $x \in \phi(M)$.
Proof: The proof follows immediately from the fact that free variables may only disappear but can never be introduced by any contraction.

Lemma 2.2 For any variable x and λ-expression P we have $(\lambda x.P)x \Rightarrow P$.
Proof: This can be shown by induction on the construction of P. Namely,

---

$(\lambda x.x)x \Rightarrow x$ by $\beta 1$

$(\lambda x.y)x \Rightarrow y$ by $\beta 2$

$(\lambda x.\lambda x.E)x \Rightarrow \lambda x.E$ by $\beta 3$

$(\lambda x.\lambda y.E)x \Rightarrow \lambda y.(\lambda x.E)x$ by $\beta 4$, if x and y are different, where $(\lambda x.E)x \Rightarrow E$ by the induction hypothesis.

Finally, $(\lambda x.(E_1)E_2)x \Rightarrow ((\lambda x.E_1)x)(\lambda x.E_2)x \Rightarrow (E_1)E_2$ by $\beta 5$ and by the induction hypothesis.

Lemma 2.3 If $x \notin \phi(P)$ then for every Q we have $(\lambda x.P)Q \Rightarrow P$.
Proof: Again we use structural induction. If P is a variable y then it must be different from x and thus, the assertion follows from $\beta 2$. If P has the form $\lambda y.E$ then either y is identical to x and thus, $(\lambda x.\lambda x.E)x \Rightarrow \lambda x.E$ by $\beta 3$, or else y is different from x, and $x \notin \phi(E)$, which imply that

$(\lambda x.\lambda y.E)Q \Rightarrow \lambda y.(\lambda x.E)Q \Rightarrow \lambda y.E$

by $\beta 4$ and by the induction hypothesis.

For $P \equiv (E_1)E_2$ the assertion follows from $\beta 5$ and the induction hypothesis and this completes the proof.

Lemma 2.4 For every x, z and P such that z is neither free nor bound in P we have $(\lambda x.P)z \Rightarrow \{z/x\}P$.
Proof: Again we use structural induction. If P is a variable then the assertion is trivial.
For $P \equiv \lambda x.E$ we get

$(\lambda x.\lambda x.E)z \Rightarrow \lambda x.E \Rightarrow \lambda z.(\lambda x.E)z \Rightarrow \lambda z.\{z/x\}E \equiv \{z/x\}\lambda x.E$

by the induction hypothesis and by Definitions 2.7 and 2.2.
For $P \equiv \lambda y.E$, where x and z are different from y, we have

$(\lambda x\lambda y.E)z \Rightarrow \lambda y.(\lambda x.E)z \Rightarrow \lambda y.\{z/x\}E \equiv \{z/x\}\lambda y.E.$

For $P \equiv (E_1)E_2$ the result follows immediately from $\beta 5$ and from the induction hypothesis and this completes the proof.

Corollary: If $M \cong N$ then $M \Rightarrow N$ is valid in the sense of Definition 2.7.

Proof: It suffices to consider the case when $M \rightarrow_a N$, that is when $M \equiv \lambda x.E$ and $N \equiv \lambda z.\{z/x\}E$ for some x, z, and E. In this case we have

$$M \equiv \lambda x.E \Rightarrow \lambda z.(\lambda x.E)z \Rightarrow \lambda z.\{z/x\}E \equiv N$$

by the new α-rule and by Lemma 2.4, which completes the proof.

This means that the renaming operation can be implemented by the new reduction rules. Next, we show that the same is true for the substitution operation.

Lemma 2.5 $(\lambda x.P)Q \Rightarrow [Q/x]P$ in the sense of Definition 2.7 for every x, P, and Q.

Proof: Here we use induction on the number of occurrences of variables in P.

    Basis: If P has a single occurrence of a variable then the assertion follows immediately from $\beta 1$ or $\beta 2$, and from Definition 2.4.

    Induction step: Assume that the assertion is true for all λ-expressions with at most n occurrences of variables and let P have n+1 of them. Then P has the form either $(P_1)P_2$ or $\lambda x.E$. For the former case the result follows immediately from the induction hypothesis. For $P \equiv \lambda x.E$ we have three subcases:

Case 1: x *is the same as* y. In this case the assertion is trivial.

Case 2: x *and* y *are different and* y $\notin \phi(Q)$. Here we have

$$(\lambda x.\lambda y.E)Q \Rightarrow \lambda y.(\lambda x.E)Q \Rightarrow \lambda y.[Q/x]E \cong [Q/x]\lambda y.E$$

by $\beta 4$, the induction hypothesis, and Definition 2.4.

Case 3: x *and* y *are different and* y $\in \phi(Q)$. In this case we get

$$(\lambda x.\lambda y.E)Q \Rightarrow (\lambda x.\lambda z.(\lambda y.E)z)Q \Rightarrow \lambda z.(\lambda x.(\lambda y.E)z)Q \Rightarrow$$

$$\lambda z.(\lambda x.\{z/y\}E)Q \Rightarrow \lambda z.[Q/x]\{z/y\}E \cong [Q/x]\lambda y.E$$

by α, $\beta 4$, Lemma 2.5, the induction hypothesis, and Definition 2.4. Here we have assumed that $\{z/y\}E$ has at most as many occurrences of variables as does E. This is easy to show by a separate induction and this completes the proof.

Note that neither substitution nor α-congruence is needed in our new system, since they are covered by *reduction* as defined in Definition 2.7. We can summarize the result of this section in the following theorem.

Theorem 2.3 For any two λ-expressions, M and N, if M $\Rightarrow$ N holds with respect to Definition 2.5 then it also holds with respect to Definition 2.7.

Proof: It is enough to show that M $\Rightarrow$ N holds with respect to Definition 2.7 whenever M $\cong$ N or M $\rightarrow$ N is an instance of the original β-rule. In the first case the result follows from the Corollary of Lemma 2.4 while in the second case it follows from Lemma 2.5.

The converse of Theorem 2.3 is obviously false. For instance,

$$\lambda x.E \Rightarrow \lambda z.(\lambda x.E)z$$

is not true with respect to Definition 2.5. Similarly,

$$(\lambda x.(P_1)P_2)Q \Rightarrow ((\lambda x.P_1)Q)(\lambda x.P_2)Q$$

follows immediately from Definition 2.7, but it is not so when Definition 2.5 is used.

Equality, however, is the same in both systems. In particular, both

$$(\lambda x.(P_1)P_2)Q \quad \text{and} \quad ((\lambda x.P_1)Q)(\lambda x.P_2)Q$$

are reducible to $([Q/x]P_1)[Q/x]P_2$ regardless of which definition of $\Rightarrow$ is used. Hence, they are equal in both senses. This leads to the following corollary which is an immediate consequence of the above theorem.

Corollary: The Church–Rosser theorem is true also for the new system.

The new reduction rules appear to be very convenient for computer implementations. A variant of this system is used in the implementation discussed in Chapter 6.

Exercises

2.1 Reduce the following λ-expressions to their respective normal forms using the β-rule of Section 2.3.

(a) $(((\lambda f.\lambda x.\lambda y.(x)(f)y)p)q)r$

(b) $(((\lambda x.\lambda y.\lambda z.(y)x)(x)y)(u)z)y$

(c) $(\lambda x.(\lambda y.(x)(y)y)\lambda z.(x)(z)z)(\lambda u.\lambda v.u)w$

(d) $(((\lambda x.\lambda y.\lambda z.((x)z)(y)z)(\lambda u.\lambda v.u)w)\lambda s.s)t$

(e) $(((\lambda x.(\lambda y.(x)(y)y)\lambda y.(x)(y)y)\lambda z.\lambda u.\lambda v.(u)(z)v)(\lambda r.\lambda s.r.)t)w$

2.2 Show that $[z/x]P \cong \{z/x\}P$ for every x, z, and P such that z is neither free nor bound in P. Hint: Examine the proof of Lemma 2.4.

2.3 Use induction on the construction of E to prove that

$$\lambda z.[Q/x]\{z/y\}E \cong \lambda v.[Q/x]\{v/y\}E$$

for any λ-expressions E and Q, and variables x, y, z, and v provided that both z and v satisfy the conditions for z in part (5) of Definition 2.4.

2.4 Which of the following two equations is correct?

$$((\lambda u.\lambda v.(v)u)\lambda x.(x)x)\lambda y.(y)(y)y = (\lambda v.(\lambda u.(u)v)\lambda x.(x)x)\lambda y.(y)(y)y$$

$$((\lambda v.\lambda u.(u)v)\lambda y.(y)(y)y)\lambda x.(x)x = ((\lambda u.\lambda v.(v)v)u)\lambda y.(y)(y)y$$

2.5 Consider the conventional definition of substitution:

    (1) $[Q/x]x \equiv Q$

    (2) $[Q/x]y \equiv y$

    (3) $[Q/x]\lambda x.E \equiv \lambda x.E$

    (4) $[Q/x]\lambda y.E \equiv \lambda y.[Q/x]E$ if $x \not\equiv y$; and $y \notin \phi(Q)$ or
        $x \notin \phi(E)$.

    (5) $[Q/x]\lambda y.E \equiv \lambda z.[Q/x][z/y]E$ if $x \not\equiv y$; and $y \in \phi(Q)$ and
        $x \in \phi(E)$, where z is the first variable (in the infinite
        sequence of all variables) which is not free in (E)Q.

    (6) $[Q/x](E_1)E_2 \equiv ([Q/x]E_1)[Q/x]E_2$

Show that for every E, Q, and x the result of the conventional substitution, $[Q/x]E$, is α-congruent with the result obtained from Definition 2.4.

2.6 Design and implement an algorithm to decide the α-congruence of two λ-expressions being in normal form.

CHAPTER THREE

COMBINATORS AND CONSTANT SYMBOLS

3.1 Lambda-expressions without free variables

The meaning (or the value) of a λ-expression may depend on the meaning of its free variables. The latter are determined by the *context* in which the λ-expression occurs. Formally a **context** is defined as a λ-expression with one or more *holes* in it. Each *hole* must be a proper part of the context and it must be replaceable by any λ-expression. This means that the *hole* is syntactically a λ-expression and thus, it cannot occupy the place of a missing λ or some other component which is not a legitimate λ-expression by itself.

Using a λ-expression in some context means using it as a subexpression of another expression. But, because of the possible bindings in the context, free occurrences of variables may get captured in the process. If, for example, we put the λ-expression

$\lambda x.(y)x$

in the context

$((\lambda x.\lambda y.hole)E)F$

then we get

$((\lambda x.\lambda y.\lambda x.(y)x)E)F$

which reduces to

$\lambda x.(F)x$

The free occurrence of y in $\lambda x.(y)x$ becomes bound in the given context, hence, it gets replaced by F.

Notice the difference between using an expression E in some context C, and the substitution of E for *hole* regarded as a free variable in C. The second corresponds to the application

$(\lambda hole.C)E \rightarrow [E/hole]C$

where free variables cannot be captured.

The free variables of a λ-expression correspond to the *global variables* used in a nested block or in the body of a procedure declaration in a conventional programming language. A bound variable, on the other hand, corresponds to a *formal parameter* or a *local variable*. A well-known reason for avoiding the use of global variables in conventional languages is to minimize the influence of the uncontrollable context on the behavior of a procedure.

λ-expressions having no free variables are clearly independent of their context. Indeed, they behave the same way in any context and thus, they are similar to constant symbols. Take, for example, the λ-expression $\lambda x.x$. If we apply this to some other expression we always get the other expression as a result regardless of the context. Thus, the expression $\lambda x.x$ represents the identity transformation in any context.

Definition 3.1 λ-expressions without free variables are called *closed λ-expressions* or **combinators**.

The term 'combinator' refers to their use as higher-order functions which would form new functions by combining given ones. Many of the combinators have special names. For example, the above mentioned *identity combinator* is denoted by **I** which is considered a constant symbol (or reserved word) and not a variable.

Note that the **I** combinator represents a whole class of α-congruent λ-expressions, because the λ-expression $\lambda v.v$ is an identity mapping for every variable v. This means that the **I** combinator is defined only up to α-congruence, namely

$\mathbf{I} \cong \lambda x.x$

For another example, consider the operation of function composition. Observe the fact that lambda-calculus has only two fundamental operations, application and abstraction, but no composition. Nevertheless, the composition of two functions, f and g, can be expressed in lambda-notation simply by

$\lambda x.(f)(g)x$

where x ∉ $\phi(f) \cup \phi(g)$. Hence, the combinator

compose $\cong \lambda f.\lambda g.\lambda x.(f)(g)x$

represents the composition operator. Note that this is a *Curried* operator rather than an infix one. With the aid of the conversion rules we can show that it is associative, that is

((**compose**)((**compose**)f)g)h = ((**compose**)f)((**compose**)g)h

The reader is recommended to work out the details.

Special symbols for combinators like **I** and **compose** can be treated in lambda-calculus in two different ways:

(1) Either we can use them simply as shorthands for the corresponding λ-expressions, in which case no extra reduction rules are needed for them, because we can always revert to the pure lambda-notation and use the α- and β-rules as necessary.

(2) Or else we can treat them as atoms, i.e. constant symbols, which cannot be further analyzed. Then, we have to introduce specific reduction rules to define their properties.

In this book we shall use both of these alternatives according to our needs. The defining property of the identity combinator is, of course,

(**I**)E → E

for every λ-expression E. Similarly, the composition combinator can be defined by the reduction rule

(((**compose**)F)G)E → (F)(G)E

for arbitrary λ-expressions, F, G and E.

Two other important combinators should be mentioned here, which represent the truth values in lambda-notation. Namely, the combinators **true** and **false** will be defined as follows:

true $\cong$ λx.λy.x

false $\cong$ λx.λy.y

Alternatively, they can be defined by the following reduction rules:

((**true**)P)Q → P

((**false**)P)Q → Q

for every P and Q. The reason behind these definitions is the fact that the truth values are normally used for selecting either one of two given alternatives. (Think of an IF-statement in a programming language.) If the condition evaluates to **true** then the first alternative is computed, if it evaluates to **false** then the second. Hence, the conditional expression

if C *then* P *else* Q

will take the form

((C)P)Q

in our lambda-notation. Here P and Q represent arbitrary λ-expressions, while the λ-expression C is supposed to be reducible either to λx.λy.x or to λx.λy.y. Thus, the conditional expression is represented by the combinator

λc.λp.λq.((c)p)q

which takes three arguments. Observe the fact that this combinator can be applied to arbitrary λ-expressions regardless of the 'type' of the first argument. In this respect type-free λ-calculus is similar to the machine code of a conventional computer where arbitrary operations can be performed on any data. We may get some unexpected results but that is not the computer's fault.

Returning to the combinators we can say that there are quite a few interesting and useful combinators. Some of them will be studied more thoroughly in this chapter, but we cannot discuss them all. Historically, combinators were invented first by Schoenfinkel in the late 20's. He used them to eliminate all variables from mathematical logic. Curry, who independently discovered them in about the same time, was mainly responsible for the subsequent development of their theory. Combinators have received a great deal of attention lately in computer science especially in the context of functional programming.

Exercises

3.1 Negation can be represented by the combinator **not** which is α-congruent to

$\lambda x.((x)\textbf{false})\textbf{true}$

Find combinators to represent the boolean operations **and** and **or**.

3.2 Show that the operations represented by your **and** and **or** combinators are both commutative and associative. Also, show that your **and** and **or** combinators do have the usual distributive properties.

3.3 Find a combinator to represent the prefix **apply** operator characterized by the reduction rule

$((\textbf{apply})A)B \rightarrow (A)B$

for arbitrary λ-expressions A and B. Using your representation show that also the iteration

$(((\textbf{apply})\textbf{apply})A)B$

β-reduces to (A)B.

3.2 Arithmetic and other constants and combinators

As we have seen in the previous section, both the truth values and the standard boolean operations can be represented by certain combinators, that is, by certain λ-expressions without free variables. It seems only natural that no free variables occur in these representations, since they must not depend on the context in which they are used. In other words, they must behave the same in every context. In this respect, there is no difference between a constant value like **true** or **false** and some well-defined function like **and**. As a matter of fact, every well-defined function can be considered a constant entity regardless of the number of operands it takes.

Observe the fact that even the truth values are represented here as functions. Each of them can take up to two arguments as can be seen from their representations. But that is quite natural. If we do not use constant symbols in our lambda-notation then we have only application, abstraction, and variables. So, the only way to represent context independent behavior is by using combinators.

It is important to note that almost anything can be represented in this manner. To support this claim, we show the combinator representation of natural numbers developed by A. Church. These combinators are called *Church numerals*, and they are defined as follows:

$0 \cong \lambda f.\lambda x.x$

$1 \cong \lambda f.\lambda x.(f)x$

$2 \cong \lambda f.\lambda x.(f)(f)x$

$3 \cong \lambda f.\lambda x.(f)(f)(f)x$

and, in general, the combinator representing the number n iterates its first argument to its second argument n times.

The arithmetic operations on these numerals can be represented also by appropriate combinators. For instance, the successor function, which increments its argument by one, can be represented as

succ $\cong \lambda n.\lambda f.\lambda x.(f)((n)f)x$

Note that the names of the bound variables do not matter. Addition can be represented as

$+ \cong \lambda m.\lambda n.\lambda f.\lambda x.((m)f)((n)f)x$

while multiplication will be the same as composition, namely

$* \cong \lambda m.\lambda n.\lambda f.(m)(n)f$

The reader is recommended to work out the details and find a representation for the exponentiation m^n in this framework.

A predicate to test for zero in this representation can be given as follows:

zero $\cong \lambda n.((n)(\textbf{true})\textbf{false})\textbf{true}$

The representation of the *predecessor function*, which gives $n - 1$ for $n > 0$, and 0 for $n = 0$, is quite tricky. The idea is to represent ordered pairs in lambda-notation which would correspond somehow to $[n, n - 1]$. A possible representation of the ordered pair $[a, b]$ is the expression

$\lambda z.((z)a)b$,

which has the following properties

$(\lambda z.((z)a)b)$**true** $\Rightarrow a$

and

$(\lambda z.((z)a)b)$**false** $\Rightarrow b$

Now, in analogy with the successor function we can define a function *next* to obtain $[n + 1, n]$ from $[n, n - 1]$. The corresponding λ-expression will be the following:

next $\cong \lambda p.\lambda z.((z)($**succ**$)(p)$**true**$)(p)$**true**

which makes use of only the first element of the ordered pair p representing the argument. So, we can start with $[0, 0]$ and iterate the *next* function n times to get $[n, n - 1]$. But, that is easy since the Church numeral representing the number n involves precisely n iterations. Therefore, we can apply this Church numeral to *next* as its first argument and to the expression

$\lambda z.((z)0)0$

as its second argument. This gives us the λ-expression

$((n)\lambda p.\lambda z.((z)($**succ**$)(p)$**true**$)(p)$**true**$)\lambda z.((z)0)0$

where **n** stands for the Church numeral representing the number n

Finally, in order to obtain the value of the predecessor function, we have to select the second element of the resulting ordered pair. Thus, the predecessor function can be represented by the following λ-expression:

pred $\cong \lambda n.(((n)\lambda p.\lambda z.((z)($**succ**$)(p)$**true**$)(p)$**true**$) \lambda z.((z)0)0)$**false**

It may be interesting to note that Church himself could not find a representation for the predecessor function. He had just about convinced himself that the predecessor function was not lambda-definable when Kleene found a representation for it. (See page 57 in [Klee81].)

It can be shown, in general, that every recursive function of type [N→N] is lambda-definable and integer arithmetic can be faithfully embedded in pure lambda-calculus. This seems to be a useless 'tour de force', because the decimal notation is clearly more convenient than these encoded 'numerals'. There is, however, a good reason behind this exercise. It has, indeed, some important theoretical implications. First of all, the proof of the Church–Rosser theorem extends to the arithmetic of natural numbers. Therefore, we can use the decimal notation for the natural numbers and various constant symbols for their operations knowing that the extended system still has the Church–Rosser property. Of course, we cannot say the same about real arithmetic.

The natural numbers can be represented in lambda-calculus in many different ways. The representation of their operations will have to be changed accordingly. An alternative numeral system is given in Exercise 3.6.

It should be emphasized that the *Church numerals* as well as the representations of their basic operations are all combinators. These combinators will be given special names and will be treated as *constant symbols* in the rest of this book. In fact, *we will use integers and real numbers in decimal notation as part of our lambda-notation* and we will assume that the standard arithmetic operations are implemented directly rather than via combinators. A similar assumption is made regarding the truth values and the boolean operators. So, the syntax of λ-expressions will be extended by the following.

ADDITIONAL SYNTAX RULES FOR CONSTANTS

<constant>::= <number> | <operator> | <combinator>

<number>::= <integer> | <real number>

<operator>::= <arithmetic operator> | <relational operator> |

                <predicate> | <boolean operator>

<arithmetic operator>::= + | - | * | / | **succ** | **pred** | **mod**

<relational operator>::= < | ≤ | = | ≥ | > | ≠

<predicate> ::= **zero**

<boolean operator>::= **and** | **or** | **not**

<combinator>::= **true** | **false**

All these constants will have their usual meaning. The binary operations and the relations are Curried, however, so that we write $((+)a)b$ instead of $a + b$, and $((<)a)b$ instead of $a < b$, etc. The translation to and from the usual infix notation is straightforward. The semantics of these constants will be described in more detail in Chapter 5 with the aid of their specific reduction rules.

Exercises

3.4 Define a combinator **square** to compute n^2 for a natural number n using *Church numerals*.

3.5 Find a λ-expression to represent the predicate *even* which returns **true** whenever the argument is an even number and returns **false** when it is an odd number. Use *Church numerals* and do not worry about the value of the predicate for non-numeric arguments.

3.6 Consider the following numerals:

$0 \cong \mathbf{I}$

$1 \cong \lambda z.((z)\mathbf{false})\mathbf{I}$

$2 \cong \lambda z.((z)\mathbf{false})\lambda z.((z)\mathbf{false})\mathbf{I}$

and so on. Find λ-expressions to represent the *successor* and the *predecessor* functions and the predicate to test for *zero*. The latter may be used in the definition of the *predecessor* function.

3.3 Recursive definitions and the Y combinator

Recursive functions can be defined easily in high-level programming languages such as Pascal or LISP. Therefore, they should be definable in lambda-calculus, as well. As a matter of fact, it is easy to find a formal solution to every recursion equation in lambda-calculus. This can be done with the aid of the **Y** combinator, which has the following property:

$(Y)E = (E)(Y)E$

for every λ-expression E. This implies that

$(Y)E = (E)(E)...(E)(Y)E$

for any number of iterations of E. The question is whether we can find a closed λ-expression with this property. In Chapter 2 we have seen that the λ-expression

$(\lambda x.(x)x)\lambda x.(x)x$

reduces to itself and thus, it gives rise to an infinite reduction. This feature is very similar to what we are looking for, only we need to deposit a prefix of the form (E) in each reduction step. But this can be achieved by the following modification:

$\lambda y.(\lambda x.(y)(x)x)\lambda x.(y)(x)x$

Indeed, if we apply this combinator to a λ-expression E then we get

$(\lambda x.(E)(x)x)\lambda x.(E)(x)x \Rightarrow (E)(\lambda x.(E)(x)x)\lambda x.(E)(x)x$

$\Rightarrow (E)(E)(\lambda x.(E)(x)x)\lambda x.(E)(x)x$

and so forth ad infinitum. So, the Y combinator will be defined as

$Y \cong \lambda y.(\lambda x.(y)(x)x)\lambda x.(y)(x)x$

The usefulness of this combinator is due to the fact that every recursive definition can be brought to the form of a fixed-point equation

$f = (E)f$

where f does not occur free inside E. The solution to this equation, namely the fixed-point of the higher order function E can be obtained as $(Y)E$. Indeed, the substitution of $(Y)E$ for f in the above equation yields

$(Y)E = (E)(Y)E$

which is true for every E by the definition of Y. Therefore, the Y combinator is a universal fixed-point finder, hence, it is called a *fixed-point combinator*.

In order to see how it works in a simple case consider, for example, the following definition of the factorial function.

(fact)n = *if* n=0 *then* 1 *else*((*)n)(fact)(**pred**)n

The solution of this implicit equation can be obtained in explicit form as follows. The equation is written in our lambda-notation as

(fact)n = (((**zero**)n)1)((*)n)(fact)(**pred**)n

which is equivalent to

fact = λn.(((**zero**)n)1)((*)n)(fact)(**pred**)n

Now, if we 'abstract out' (in analogy with factoring out) the free occurrences of the function name 'fact' on the right-hand side, we get

fact = (λf.λn.(((**zero**)n)1)((*)n)(f)(**pred**)n)fact

which means that fact is a fixed point of the expression

λf.λn.(((**zero**)n)1)((*)n)(f)(**pred**)n

Hence, we get the explicit form

fact = (**Y**)λf.λn.(((**zero**)n)1)((*)n)(f)(**pred**)n

which is again a combinator.

The same technique is applicable to every recursive definition regardless of the form of the expression on the right-hand side. This means that in lambda-calculus we have a universal recursion-removal technique that always works. This broad generality, however, does have its problems as it produces a formal solution even if the given fixed-point equation has no realistic solution. Take, for example, the

x = x + 1

which has obviously no finite solution because the *successor* function has no fixed points. Nevertheless, the fixed-point combinator would yield a formal solution in the following closed form:

x = (**Y**)λx.((+)x)1

Here the right-hand side gives rise to an infinte reduction, which yields an infinite number of iterations, because it has no normal form. Indeed, the

Y combinator converts every recursion into an iteration, but it cannot terminate the iteration by itself.

The existence of a universal fixed-point combinator in type-free lambda-calculus has serious consequences as manifested by the following:

Curry's paradox: The usual logical properties of *implication* are inconsistent with β-equality.

Proof: The implication operator ⊃ must satisfy the following axiom written in conventional notation:

$$(P \supset (P \supset Q)) \supset (P \supset Q)$$

Furthermore, it must satisfy the inference rule of *modus ponens*, which says that

if both P *and* (P ⊃ Q) *are true then so is* Q

Let **imp** denote the Curried version of ⊃. Then the above axiom will be written as

$$((\textbf{imp})((\textbf{imp})P)((\textbf{imp})P)Q)((\textbf{imp})P)Q$$

For arbitrary Q, let N be defined as

$$N = \lambda x.((\textbf{imp})x)((\textbf{imp})x)Q$$

and let

$$P = (\textbf{Y})N$$

be a fixed point of N. Hence, we get

$$((\textbf{imp})P)((\textbf{imp})P)Q = (N)P = (N)(\textbf{Y})N = P$$

By substitution in the axiom we get

$$((\textbf{imp})((\textbf{imp})P)((\textbf{imp})P)Q)((\textbf{imp})P)Q =$$

$$((\textbf{imp})P)((\textbf{imp})P)Q = P$$

Now, since the axiom must be true for any P and Q,

$$P = (\textbf{Y})N = \textbf{true}$$

must be the case for any Q (which is used in the definition of N). But then from *modus ponens* and from the axiom we can conclude that

$$Q = \textbf{true}$$

for arbitrary Q, which is clearly a paradox.

One might suggest that the problem with the **Y** combinator is due to the fact that it involves self-application. Clearly, the application of a function to itself seems inconsistent with the fact that the cardinality of the function space R^D is always greater than that of D. Therefore, it is impossible to find a reasonable domain D and a range R such that $R^D \subset D$ as implied by self-application. But, if the function space is restricted to Scott-continuous functions then one can construct such domains. This means that self-application by itself is not inconsistent with set theory, but the usability of the type-free lambda-calculus has certain limitations.

Self-application may be useful for certain purposes. It is quite possible to apply a computer program to itself and get a meaningful result. A well known example is a LISP interpreter written in LISP. Also, one can easily write self-applicable programs in the machine code of a regular computer. Indeed, for a truly type-free theory of functions self-application cannot be ruled out.

Note that the universal applicability of the **Y** combinator does not offer a practical solution to every fixed-point equation. If, for instance, we were to solve the perfectly reasonable fixed-point equation

$$x = 3x - 10$$

that is

$$x = ((-)((*)3)x)10$$

then we would get

$$x = (\lambda x.((-)((*)3)x)10)x$$

and the explicit form

$$x = (\textbf{Y})\lambda x.((-)((*)3)x)10$$

The right-hand side of this equation reduces to

$$(\lambda x.((-)((*)3)x)10)(\textbf{Y})\lambda x.((-)((*)3)x)10$$

which further reduces to

$$((-)((*)3)(\textbf{Y})\lambda x.((-)((*)3)x)10)10$$

and so on indefinitely. The right-hand side has no normal form so we cannot get a finite result from this infinite development.

In case of a well-founded recursion, however, the iteration generated by the **Y** combinator will terminate precisely at the right moment. For instance, the application of the explicit form of the factorial function to the argument 5 would yield the result in precisely 5 iterations. This is due to the presence of a second abstraction, i.e. the prefix λn, and the predicate **zero**.

Unfortunately, it is in general undecidable whether a recursively defined function is computable in a finite number of steps (i.e. has a normal form) when applied to some argument. The fact that there exist unsolvable equations should not be a surprise. It is also reasonable that we cannot have an algorithm to recognize them mechanically.

For the sake of completeness we have to mention that there are other fixed-point combinators besides the best known **Y** combinator. The following was given by Turing:

$$\mathbf{T} \cong (\lambda x.\lambda y.(y)((x)x)y)\lambda x.\lambda y.(y)((x)x)y$$

It is easy to see that

$$(\mathbf{T})E \Rightarrow (E)(\mathbf{T})E$$

for every λ-expression E. Actually, there is an infinite sequence of fixed-point combinators $Y_1, Y_2, \dots$ where

$$Y_1 \cong \mathbf{Y}$$

$$Y_2 \cong (Y_1)\mathbf{G}$$

and in general

$$Y_{n+1} \cong (Y_n)\mathbf{G}$$

where

$$\mathbf{G} \cong \lambda x.\lambda y.(y)(x)y$$

The reader should verify that $Y_2 \Rightarrow \mathbf{T}$, where **T** is the fixed-point combinator of Turing. For more details see exercise **3.9**

Exercises

3.7 Give a recursive definition for the Fibonacci numbers and use the **Y** combinator to compute the fifth Fibonacci number, i.e. the value of (*Fibonacci*)5.

3.8 Give a recursive definition for the greatest common divisor of two integers and compute the value of ((gcd)10)14 using the **Y** combinator.

3.9 Consider the sequence of combinators Y_1, Y_2, ... , and the combinator **G** as defined at the end of this section. Show that

    (a) Each Y_n is a fixed-point combinator;

    (b) Each Y_n is a fixed-point of **G**, i.e. $Y_n = (G)Y_n$,

which means that **G** has an infinite number of fixed-points each of which is a fixed-point combinator.

3.4 Elimination of bound variables: bracket abstraction

According to a fundamental theorem of Schönfinkel and Curry, *the entire lambda-calculus can be recast in the theory of combinators which has only one basic operation: application.* Abstraction is represented in this theory with the aid of two distinguished combinators: **S** and **K**, which are called **standard combinators**. The idea is similar to the representation of composition in terms of application and abstraction, but here we have a much more difficult task.

First, we should observe the fact that abstraction is actually a *partial inverse* of the application. We have, namely

    $(\lambda x.P)x \Rightarrow P$

for every λ-expression P and variable x. But the order of these two operations is important here. If we use them in the reverse order, i.e. if we first apply P to x and then abstract the result with respect to x, then we get

    $\lambda x.(P)x$

which is clearly not β-reducible to P. (The prefix λx. will not disappear unless the entire expression is applied to some other expression.) Even so, P may have some free occurrences of x which get captured by the prefix λx. Therefore, the application

$$(\lambda x.(P)x)Q$$

reduces to $([Q/x]P)Q$ which is, in general, different from $(P)Q$. Of course, we can fix this problem by using a fresh variable for the abstraction. Namely, it is easy to prove the following:

> **Lemma 3.1** For any λ-expressions, P and Q, and a variable x such that x $\notin \phi(P)$ we have
>
> $$(\lambda x.(P)x)Q \Rightarrow (P)Q$$

This means, that for x $\notin \phi(P)$ the expression λx.(P)x is extensionally equal to P, although it has a different normal form. In other words, our α- and β-rules are insufficient for proving the equality

$$\lambda x.(P)x = P \quad \text{for } x \notin \phi(P)$$

although these two expressions represent the same *extensional* function.

Remember that two functions are called extensionally equal if they have the same value for all arguments. In symbols,

$$f = g \quad \text{iff} \quad (f)x = (g)x \quad \text{for all x.}$$

Now, in order to make our lambda-calculus *extensionally complete* we have to introduce a new reduction rule as follows:

THE ETA-RULE

(η) λx.(P)x $\rightarrow$ P whenever x $\notin \phi(P)$

By adding this rule to our axiom system we can extend the notion of β-equality to extensional equality, which is then formally defined as $\beta\eta$-equality.

However, for the most part of the development of our theory, the η-rule is not necessary. Therefore, we will continue to use only the α- and the β-rules as our standard tools for evaluating λ-expressions, and every application of the η-rule will be made explicit.

Returning to the question of eliminating abstraction by using combinators instead, the number of permissible combinators is a critical issue. If we allow an arbitrary number of different combinators then the problem becomes much simpler. Every λ-expression without free variables can be considered a combinator, so it can be used as such. (There is a certain analogy with the elimination of division via multiplication by the inverse of the divisor.) Free variables, on the other hand, can be 'abstracted out' from any λ-expression. If, for instance, u and v are the only free variables in P then

$$\lambda u.\lambda v.P$$

is clearly a combinator with

$$((\lambda u.\lambda v.P)u)v = P$$

This way we can replace every λ-expression by an equivalent one having only constants, combinators, and free variables applied to each other. This gives rise to the notion of a *combinator expression* which is defined by the following simplified syntax.

THE SYNTAX OF COMBINATOR EXPRESSIONS

<combinator expression>::=<atom>|<application>

<atom>::=<variable>|<constant>|<combinator>

<application>::=(<combinator expression>)<combinator expression>

Next we shall prove that the two standard combinators, **S** and **K**, are sufficient for eliminating all abstractions, i.e. all bound variables from every λ-expression. These combinators are defined as follows.

$$\mathbf{S} \cong \lambda x.\lambda y.\lambda z.((x)z)(y)z$$

$$\mathbf{K} \cong \lambda x.\lambda y.x.$$

Note that the **K** combinator is actually the same as **true**. Furthermore, the identity combinator

$$\mathbf{I} \cong \lambda x.x$$

can be expressed in terms of **S** and **K** due to the following equality:

$$((\mathbf{S})\mathbf{K})\mathbf{K} = \mathbf{I}$$

which can be easily verified by the reader. Hence, we can use these three combinators **S**, **K**, and **I** where **I** is just a shorthand for **((S)K)K**.

A combinator expression in which the only combinators are the standard ones is called a standard combinator expression.

In order to eliminate the bound variables from a λ-expression we use an operation called **bracket abstraction**, which is the combinatory equivalent of λ-abstraction. Namely, for every variable x and standard combinator expression M there exists a standard combinator expression [x]M such that [x]M = λx.M. Note that the bracket prefix, [x], is only a meta-notation and the expression [x]M stands for a true standard combinator expression which is β-convertible to λx.M.

ALGORITHM FOR BRACKET ABSTRACTION

Input: A variable x and a standard combinator expression M.

Output: A standard combinator expression [x]M with [x]M = λx.M.

The algorithm proceeds as follows:
    If M ≡ c where c is a constant then let [x]M = **(K)**c.
    If M = C where C is one of the standard combinators then let [x]M = **(K)**C.
    If M ≡ v where v is a variable then let [x]M = **I** for v ≡ x, and let [x]M = **(K)**v for v ≢ x.
    Finally, if M = (P)Q for some standard combinator expressions, P and Q, then let [x]M = **((S)**[x]P)[x]Q.

The last clause of the algorithm shows that it must be applied recursively until we get down to the atomic components. It is easy to verify that the expression [x]M obtained from this algorithm is indeed equal to λx.M. For that purpose we use induction on the construction of M. The assertion is trivial when M is an atom or a standard combinator. If M is an application then we have

$$((S)[x]P)[x]Q = ((S)\lambda x.P)\lambda x.Q$$

from the induction hypothesis. Here the right-hand side β-reduces to

$$\lambda z.((\lambda x.P)z)(\lambda x.Q)z$$

by the definition of **S**. This further reduces to

$$\lambda z.(\{z/x\}P)\{z/x\}Q = \lambda z.\{z/x\}(P)Q = \lambda x.(P)Q$$

according to Lemma 2.4, Definition 2.2, and the α-rule, which completes the proof.

Theorem 3.1 To every λ-expression E one can find a standard combinator expression F such that E = F.

Proof: Given an arbitrary λ-expression, E, we successively eliminate its bound variables by performing bracket abstraction inside-out. This means that we apply our algorithm to the innermost abstractions (if any) occurring in E. Thereby we get some E′ such that E′ = E and there are fewer abstractions in E′ than in E. Repeating this process with E′ in place of E, eventually we get a standard combinator expression F = E.

Example: Consider the following λ-expression:

$$((\lambda x.\lambda y.(x)(y)y\lambda z.(x)(z)z)(\lambda u.\lambda v.u)w$$

Applying the algorithm to the innermost λ's yields

$$((\lambda x.((S)[y]x)[y](y)y)((S)[z]x)[z](z)z)(\lambda u.(K)u)w$$

which is equal to

$$((\lambda x.((S)(K)x)((S)I)I)((S)(K)x)((S)I)I)(((S)[u]K)[u]u)w.$$

Next we get

$$(((((S)[x](S)(K)x)[x]((S)I)I)((S)(K)x)((S)I)I)(((S)(K)K)I)w$$

and eventually

$$(((((S)((S)(K)S)((S)(K)K)I)((S)((S)(K)S)(K)I)(K)I)((S)(K)x)((S)I)I)$$
$$(((S)(K)K)I)w$$

which is equal to our original λ-expression. By the way, the normal form of this expression is

$$(x)(w)w$$

An immediate consequence of the above theorem is the following:

Corollary: Every closed λ-expression is equal to some standard combinator expression with no variables in it.

As can be seen from the previous example, the size of the expression grows larger and larger with each subsequent abstraction. Therefore, the above algorithm is impractical when we have to abstract on a large number of variables.

Curry improved on the basic algorithm by introducing two more combinators, **B** and **C**, for the following special cases of **S**.

$$\mathbf{B} \cong \lambda x.\lambda y.\lambda z.(x)(y)z$$

$$\mathbf{C} \cong \lambda x.\lambda y.\lambda z.((x)z)y$$

Having these combinators we can simplify the expressions obtained from the basic algorithm by applying the following rules:

(1) $((S)(K)P)(K)Q = (K)(P)Q$

(2) $((S)(K)P)I = P$ (η)

(3) $((S)(K)P)Q = ((B)P)Q$

(4) $((S)P)(K)Q = ((C)P)Q$

It is interesting to note that the second rule can only be derived in lambda-calculus by using the η-rule, as well. This means that the second equation is an *extensional* one in lambda-calculus. The reader should verify each of these equalities.

The improved version of the abstraction algorithm will follow the same steps as the basic algorithm but whenever an expression of the form $((S)P)Q$ is created it will be simplified using the above equations, if it is possible to do so. For that purpose, the equations will be considered in the priority of their sequence, that is, if more than one equation is applicable at the same time then the one with the smallest serial number will be applied.

To see this algorithm at work consider a function with two variables, $((F)x)y$. Abstracting on x gives us

$$[x]((F)x)y = ((S)[x](F)x)[x]y = ((S)((S)[x]F)[x]x)[x]y =$$

$$((S)((S)(K)F)I)(K)y = ((S)F)(K)y = ((C)F)y$$

Similarly, abstracting on y yields

$$[y]((F)x)y = ((S)[y](F)x)[y]y = ((S)((S)[y]F)[y]x)[y]y =$$

$$((S)((S)(K)F)(K)x)I = ((S)(K)(F)x)I = (F)x$$

This is clearly better than what we can get from the basic algorithm. Yet the size of the resulting expression may still grow too fast when repeated abstractions are made. Assume, that P and Q are λ-expressions with several free variables, say x_1, x_2, x_3, ... Then Curry's algorithm will give the following results:

$$[x_1](P)Q = ((S)[x_1]P)[x_1]Q$$

$$[x_2][x_1](P)Q = ((S)((B)S)[x_2][x_1]P)[x_2][x_1]Q$$

$$[x_3][x_2][x_1](P)Q = ((S)((B)S)((B)(B)S)[x_3][x_2][x_1]P)\ [x_3][x_2][x_1]Q$$

and so on. The size of the expression will increase as a quadratic function of the number of abstractions.

Significant further improvements were made by David Turner who introduced three more combinators, S', B', and C', which are related to S, B, and C. Their definitions are as follows:

$$S' \cong \lambda t.\lambda x.\lambda y.\lambda z.(t)((x)z)(y)z$$

$$B' \cong \lambda t.\lambda x.\lambda y.\lambda z.(t)(x)(y)z$$

$$C' \cong \lambda t.\lambda x.\lambda y.\lambda z.(t)((x)z)y$$

These new combinators behave very much like their counterparts except that they 'reach across' an extra term at the front.

TURNER'S ALGORITHM

Use the algorithm of Curry, but whenever an expression beginning with S, B, or C is formed use one of the following simplifications, if it is possible to do so.

$$((S)((B)T)P)Q = (((S')T)P)Q$$

$$((B)T)((B)P)Q = (((B')T)P)Q$$

$$((C)((B)T)P)Q = (((C')T)P)Q$$

Turner's algorithm would increase the length of an expression as a linear function of the number of abstractions. Namely,

$$[x_1](P)Q = ((S)[x_1]P)[x_1]Q$$

$$[x_2][x_1](P)Q = (((S')S)[x_2][x_1]P)[x_2][x_1]Q$$

$$[x_3][x_2][x_1](P)Q = (((S')(S')S)[x_3][x_2][x_1]P)[x_3][x_2][x_1]Q$$

and so on.

These combinators have been used in the design of the Normal Order Reduction Machine - NORMA for short - developed by the Austin Research Center of the Burroughs Corporation. Actually, the above definition of **B′** is due to Mark Scheevel, and it is slightly different from Turner's original definition, that is,

B′ $\cong \lambda t.\lambda x.\lambda y.\lambda z.((t)x)(y)z$

The modified version of **B′** is claimed to be more efficient than the original.

There are many other efforts to improve the efficiency of bracket abstraction as can be seen from the literature. It is quite interesting to see that these purely theoretical constructs have become important practical tools for such mundane purposes as hardware design.

To conclude this section we have to emphasize that the theory of combinators can be developed totally independently of lambda-calculus, in which case the combinators are defined directly by their reduction rules, i.e. by their *applicative behavior*. As we have seen, the standard combinators, **S** and **K**, are sufficient for representing arbitrary closed λ-expressions, hence, for an independent development of the theory of combinators we need only these two combinators and their reduction rules:

$$(((S)A)B)C \rightarrow ((A)C)(B)C$$

and

$$((K)A)B \rightarrow A$$

for arbitrary combinator expressions, A, B, and C.

Bracket abstraction represents a translation mechanism from the λ-notation to combinator expressions, but it is not needed for an independent development of the theory of combinators. However, if we define combinators directly by their reduction rules then their representations by closed λ-expressions may not be unique up to α-congruence. A case in point is the fixed-point combinator, which has many noncongruent representations in lambda-notation. In particular, the λ-expressions representing the combinators

$$\mathbf{Y} \cong \lambda y.(\lambda x.(y)(x)x)\lambda x.(y)(x)x$$

and

$$\mathbf{T} \cong (\lambda x.\lambda y.(y)((x)x)y)\lambda x.\lambda y.(y)((x)x)y$$

are noncongruent (and not even β-convertible), although their applicative behavior is the same. This shows that the relationship between λ-calculus and the theory of combinators is more subtle than one might think at first. A deeper analysis of this relationship can be found in [Baren81] or in [Hind86].

The intuitive appeal of the lambda-notation is certainly missing from pure combinator expressions even if we use a great deal more combinators than just the standard ones. The lack of λ-abstraction seems to be an advantage in functional programming, but a completely variable-free notation is not always desirable. More about functional programming can be found in Chapter 5.

Exercises

3.10 Show that the standard combinators, S and K, satisfy the following equalities:

$$((S)((S)(K)S)(K)K)(K)K = (K)((S)K)K$$

$$((S)((S)(K)S)((S)(K)K)K)(K)((S)K)K = K$$

and

$$((S)((S)(K)S)((S)(K)(S)(K)S)((S)(K)(S)(K)K)S)(K)(K)((S)K)K = S$$

3.11 Prove the following *extensional (i.e., $\beta\eta$)* equality:

$$((S)((S)(K)S)K)(K)((S)K)K = ((S)K)K$$

3.12 Use bracket abstraction to prove that the **Y** combinator satisfies the equality

$$\mathbf{Y} = ((S)((S)A)B)((S)A)B$$

where

$$A = ((S)(K)S)((S)(K)K)I$$

$$B = ((S)((S)(K)S)(K)I)(K)I$$

and S, K, I are the standard combinators.

3.13 Find a more compact representation of the **Y** combinator using Turner's combinators.

3.14 Find a standard combinator expression to represent Turing's fixed-point combinator **T**.

CHAPTER FOUR

LIST MANIPULATION IN LAMBDA-CALCULUS

4.1 An extension of the syntax of λ-expressions

Lists are regarded only as data structures in most programming languages. An exception is LISP where the programs themselves are structured as nested lists. This has been an important step toward a uniform treatment of programs and data. Modern functional languages, however, with the exception of Backus's FP, seem to have thrown out the baby with the bathwater by abandoning this interesting idea.

The construction of a list of functions is one of the fundamental program forming operations called 'combining forms' in FP. The irony of the situation is that this combining form would be more natural in a nonstrict language such as Miranda, which favors lazy evaluation, than it is in FP, which is strict. The implementation of Miranda is based on graph-reduction where both the program and its data are represented internally as graphs, and they are actually merged during the execution. So, it seems only natural that they may have similar structures. The implementation of functional languages using graph-reduction is the subject of an interesting book by Simon L. Peyton Jones [Peyt87]. List construction, however, is not considered as a program forming operation in that book, because in Miranda the elements of a list must be all of the same type.

Moreover, the implementation of Miranda involves a translation to the type-free lambda-calculus where the distinction between functions and arguments disappears. The same is true for ML and many other functional languages.

In contrast with those, FP makes a sharp distinction between programs and data. The latter are called *'objects'* and a list of objects is syntactically different from a list of functions. *Function lists have an interesting applicative property in FP which can facilitate parallel processing without expliciltly requiring it.* More details on FP and Miranda can be found in Chapter 5.

In this chapter we will show that a minor extension of the standard lambda-calculus makes it possible to integrate *function lists* and *data lists* in a uniform framework. Our system is fully consistent with standard lambda-calculus, which is indeed a proper part of it.

As a matter of fact, lists and list-manipulating functions can be represented in pure lambda-calculus in a fashion similar to the representation of natural numbers by Church numerals as discussed in Section 3.2. The idea of 'encoding' a list as a standard λ-expression is similar to the representation of ordered pairs which has been used for the representation of the predecessor function in Section 3.2. But, here we need an extra constant symbol, **nil**, to represent the empty list. Then a list of arbitrary λ-expressions,

$$[E_1, ..., E_n],$$

can be represented by

$$\lambda z.((z)E_1) ... \lambda z.((z)E_n)\textbf{nil}$$

where z is any variable which is not free in E_i ($1 \leq i \leq n$). For the given representation the two basic list manipulating operations can be implemented by the following combinators:

head $\cong \lambda x.(x)\textbf{true}$

tail $\cong \lambda x.(x)\textbf{false}$

Indeed, the application of **head** to the above representation of a list returns its first member E_1, while the application of **tail** returns the representation of the remaining (n-1)-element list, as can be verified easily by the reader. The so called list-constructor operator, which appends its first operand as a new element to the front of its second operand regarded as a list, can be represented by the combinator

cons $\cong \lambda x.\lambda y.\lambda z.((z)x)y$

The reader should verify that

$((\text{cons})A)[E_1, ..., E_n] \Rightarrow [A, E_1, ..., E_n]$

in view of the given representation.

This means that list manipulation can be implemented in standard lambda-calculus without using any extra notation. However, this implementation is based on a simulation of the elementary list operations via β-reduction where each of those operations takes several β-reduction steps to execute.

A more concise representation can be obtained if the list manipulating operators are treated as true combinators, i.e. atomic symbols supplied with appropriate reduction rules. Then a list of the form

$[E_1, ..., E_n],$

can be represented by

$((\text{cons})E_1)...((\text{cons})E_n)\textbf{nil}$

and the reduction rules for the **head, tail,** and **cons** combinators can be given accordingly.

Here we shall follow a similar approach, but we use a conventional notation for lists with brackets and commas. Arbitrarily nested lists will be considered as valid λ-expressions, and the elementary list operators will be treated as constant symbols. The extended syntax is given below.

THE EXTENDED SYNTAX OF λ-EXPRESSIONS

$<\lambda\text{-expression}>::=<\text{variable}> \mid <\text{constant}> \mid <\text{abstraction}> \mid$

$\qquad\qquad\qquad <\text{application}> \mid <\text{list}>$

$<\text{variable}>::=<\text{identifier}>$

$<\text{constant}>::=<\text{number}> \mid <\text{operator}> \mid <\text{combinator}>$

$<\text{abstraction}>::= \lambda<\text{variable}>.<\lambda\text{-expression}>$

<application>::= (<λ-expression>)<λ-expression>

<list>::= [<λ-expression><list-tail> | []

<list-tail>::= ,<λ-expression><list-tail> |]

<operator>::=<arithmetic operator> | <relational operator> |

        <predicate> | <boolean operator> | <list operator>

<arithmetic operator>::= + | − | * | / | **succ** | **pred** | **mod**

<relational operator>::= < | ≤ | = | ≥ | > | ≠

<predicate>::= **zero** | **null**

<boolean operator>::= **and** | **or** | **not**

<list operator>::= ∧ | ~ | &

<combinator>::= **true** | **false** | **Y**

The empty list is denoted by []. The constant symbols ∧, ~, and & represent the **head, tail,** and **cons** operators, respectively. *We use these single character symbols in our implementation simply because they are easier to type on a terminal keyboard than the corresponding four letter words.* The predicate **null** represents the test for the empty list. So, we can form λ-expressions like

    (λq.[p,q,r])S

    (λx.[(x)y,(y)x])M

    (λx.(λy.[x,y])a)[b,c,d]

With this, of course, we expect that the first expression here will reduce to [p,S,r], the second to [(M)y,(y)M], and the third to [[b,c,d],a]. To achieve this we shall need some additional reduction rules which will be given in the next section.

4.2 Additional axioms for list manipulation

First, we give the reduction rules for the elementary list operators introduced in the previous section.

Head

$$(\wedge)[] \rightarrow []$$

$$(\wedge)[E_1, ..., E_n] \rightarrow E_1 \quad \text{for } n \geq 1$$

Tail

$$(\sim)[] \rightarrow []$$

$$(\sim)[E_1, ..., E_n] \rightarrow [E_2, ..., E_n] \quad \text{for } n \geq 2$$

Construction

$$((\&)A)[] \rightarrow [A]$$

$$((\&)A)[E_1, ..., E_n] \rightarrow [A, E_1, ..., E_n] \quad \text{for } n \geq 1$$

Test for the empty list

$$(\text{null})[] \rightarrow \text{true}$$

$$(\text{null})[E_1, ..., E_n] \rightarrow \text{false} \quad \text{for } n \geq 1$$

Selection

$$(1)[E_1, ..., E_n] \rightarrow E_1 \quad \text{for } n \geq 1$$

$$(k)[E_1, ..., E_n] \rightarrow ((\text{pred})k)[E_2, ..., E_n] \quad \text{for } k > 1, n \geq 1$$

Note that A and E_i ($1 \leq i \leq n$) denote arbitrary λ-expressions in these rules. It should be emphasized that we have not defined these operations for all possible arguments. For instance, (**null**)3 is undefined, but we do not force its evaluation by replacing it by a so called *'undefined symbol'*. Such λ-expressions will simply be left alone as being irreducible, i.e. already in normal form. They may, of course, occur as subexpressions of more meaningful λ-expressions, since they may get discarded during the evaluation process.

In contrast with LISP, both ∧ and ~ are well-defined here for the empty list. This turns out to be very useful for a recursive definition of certain list-manipulating functions. The selection of the first member of a list, however, is undefined for the empty list. Hence, (1)E is not always the same as (∧)E.

The apparently meaningless application of an integer k to some list L is interpreted here as the the selection of the k-th element of L. Both the integer k and the list L may be given as arbitrary λ-expressions and thus, they must be evaluated (to some extent), before we can tell whether they fit together. If, for instance, A and B are arbitrary λ-expressions then the λ-expression

$$(2)((\&)A)(\lambda x.(\lambda y.((\&)x)y)[])B$$

reduces to (2)[A,B] and hence to B. On the other hand,

$$(3)[A,B]$$

reduces to (1)[], which is in normal form.

The selection function k should not be confused with the constant valued function λx.k, which always evaluates to k when applied to any other λ-expression.

Now, in order to make our system work we need additional reduction rules. The purpose of these new rules is to make our list structures accessible for the α-rules and β-rules. First of all, we want to distribute the renaming prefix among the elements of a list. This will be done by the α5-rule given below. The following is a complete definition of the renaming operation in terms of rewriting rules.

ALPHA-RULES

(α1) $\{z/x\}x \rightarrow z$

(α2) $\{z/x\}E \rightarrow E$ if x does not occur free in E

(α3) $\{z/x\}\lambda y.E \rightarrow \lambda y.\{z/x\}E$ for every λ-expression E, if $x \not\equiv y \not\equiv z$.

(α4) $\{z/x\}(E_1)E_2 \rightarrow (\{z/x\}E_1)\{z/x\}E_2$

(α5) $\{z/x\}[E_1,...,E_n] \rightarrow [\{z/x\}E_1,..., \{z/x\}E_n]$ for n≥0

Similarly, we can use an extra rule, $\beta5$, to implement 'pointwise' substitution in a list.

BETA RULES

($\beta1$) $(\lambda x.x)Q \to Q$

($\beta2$) $(\lambda x.E)Q \to E$ if x does not occur free in E

($\beta3$) $(\lambda x.\lambda y.E)Q \to \lambda z.(\lambda x.\{z/y\}E)Q$ if $x \not\equiv y$, and z is neither free
                                                                   nor bound in (E)Q.

($\beta4$) $(\lambda x.(E_1)E_2)Q \to ((\lambda x.E_1)Q)(\lambda x.E_2)Q$

($\beta5$) $(\lambda x.[E_1, ..., E_n])Q \to [(\lambda x.E_1)Q, ..., (\lambda x.E_n)Q]$ for $n \geq 0$

It is interesting to note that our $\beta5$-rule has a certain similarity to the applicative property of *construction* in FP, which we mentioned before. This property can be formulated in our system as the following reduction rule:

$$([E_1, ..., E_n])Q \to [(E_1)Q, ..., (E_n)Q]$$

Now, if we can distribute an abstraction prefix over a list then we can replace $\beta5$ by the above rule. That is precisely what we shall do by using the following two gamma rules instead of $\beta5$.

GAMMA-RULES

($\gamma1$) $([E_1, ..., E_n])Q \to [(E_1)Q, ..., (E_n)Q]$ for $n \geq 0$

($\gamma2$) $\lambda x.[E_1, ..., E_n] \to [\lambda x.E_1, ..., \lambda x.E_n]$ for $n \geq 0$

By adding these new axioms to the α-rules and $\beta1$ through $\beta4$ we get a complete system in which every λ-expression will be evaluated by reducing it to its normal form if such exists.

> *The definitions of reduction ($\twoheadrightarrow$) and equality ($=$) will remain the same as given in Chapter 2 except that the relation $\to$ will be defined by the new set of rules.*

To see how this system works let us consider an example. Take, for instance, the algebraic law of composition

$$[f, g] \bullet h = [f \bullet h, g \bullet h],$$

which is treated as an axiom in FP. Here we can prove this equality as follows:

$$[f, g] \bullet h = ((\lambda x.\lambda y.\lambda z.(x)(y)z)[f, g])h$$

by definition of composition as given in Section 3.1. The right-hand side β-reduces (in several steps) to $\lambda z.([f, g])(h)z$. Then by using the γ-rules we get

$$\lambda z.([f, g])(h)z \rightarrow \lambda z.[(f)(h)z, (g)(h)z] \rightarrow$$

$$[\lambda z.(f)(h)z, \lambda z.(g)(h)z] = [f \bullet h, g \bullet h]$$

which completes the proof.

The first γ-rule can be used also for selecting simultaneously more than one element of a list. Namely, for any k-tuple of integers, $[i_1, ..., i_k]$, we have

$$([i_1, ..., i_k])Q \rightarrow [(i_1)Q, ..., (i_k)Q]$$

by $\gamma 1$ for any Q. If Q is a list then this is obviously a k-fold simultaneous projection of Q.

To conclude this section we have to emphasize that lists are given certain applicative properties by the gamma-rules which do not exist in other systems. Clearly, the γ-rules do not hold for the representation of lists in pure lambda-calculus which has beeen discussed at the beginning of this Chapter. It is unlikely that there exists some other representation which satisfies the γ-rules, but we do not know for sure. A common feature of the γ-rules is that they are trying to push the brackets to the outside of the λ-expressions. This will have an impact on the so called *head normal form* in our system.

4.3 List manipulating functions

With the aid of the elementary list operators and predicates defined in the previous sections we can define other list manipulating functions. For instance, the *append* function which joins together two lists satisfies the following equation:

$$((append)[A_1, ..., A_m])[B_1, ..., B_n] = [A_1,...,A_m, B_1, ..., B_n]$$

Therefore, we can define it recursively this way:

$$((append)x)y = if(\textbf{null})x \; then \; y \; else \; ((\&)(\wedge)x)((append)(\sim)x)y$$

In pure λ-notation, i.e. without syntactic sugar, this takes the form

$$append = \lambda x.\lambda y.(((\textbf{null})x)y)((\&)(\wedge)x)((append)(\sim)x)y$$

This is a recursive equation so we will use the **Y** combinator to find its solution. Thus, we get the definition

$$append = (\textbf{Y})\lambda f.\lambda x.\lambda y.(((\textbf{null})x)y)((\&)(\wedge)x)((f)(\sim)x)y$$

This definition will be used for the computation of the value of *append* for some arguments, say, [a,b,c] and [d,e], in such a way as if we had written

$$(\lambda append.((append)[a,b,c])[d,e])(\textbf{Y})\lambda f.\lambda x.\lambda y.(((\textbf{null})x)y)$$

$$((\&)(\wedge)x)((f)(\sim)x)y$$

which would reduce to

[a,b,c,d,e]

as required.

Another important function is *map* which distributes the application of a function over a list. More precisely, it has this property:

$$((map)f)[E_1, ..., E_n] = [(f)E_1, ..., (f)E_n]$$

So, it can be defined recursively as

$$((map)f)x = if(\textbf{null})x \; then \; [] \; else \; ((\&)(f)(\wedge)x)((map)f)(\sim)x$$

Again, by using the **Y** combinator we get the explicit form

$$map = (\textbf{Y})\lambda m.\lambda f.\lambda x.(((\textbf{null})x)[])((\&)(f)(\wedge)x)((m)f)(\sim)x$$

which works exactly the way we wanted.

The continued arithmetic operations can also be treated as list oriented operations. Actually, these operations are the polyadic extensions of the usual binary operations, because they take an arbitrary number of arguments. However, in functional programming they are treated as unary functions which take only a list as an argument. The length of the list is, of course, arbitrary. Using the same trick we can define the sum of an arbitrary sequence of integers or integer valued expressions this way:

$$(sum)x = if(\textbf{null})x \; then \; 0 \; else \; ((+)(1)x)(sum)(\sim)x$$

This recursion appears to be similar to the one we have used for *map*, but it is, in fact, quite different. In the case of *map* the function f can be applied to the first member of the list without any delay. Such a recursion is called tail recursion, and it can make some progress in the evaluation before unwinding the entire recursion. In the above definition of *sum* the application of the binary addition operator + must be deferred until the end of the list is found. Therefore, it takes additional space to remember all the pending additions while going deeper and deeper into the recursion. But, we can make the definition of *sum* tail recursive by introducing an 'accumulator' parameter this way:

$$((sum)a)x = if \; (\textbf{null})x \; then \; a$$

$$else \; ((sum)((+)a)(\wedge)x)(\sim)x$$

The second argument of *sum* on the right-hand side of the equation is $(\sim)x$ which is one element shorter than x. The question is whether the first argument of *sum* is evaluated before the recursion continues. If so, then the first element of the list will be added to the accumulator before the recursion continues and thus, no addition will be pending during the recursion. Otherwise, the pending additions will have to be remembered just as before. Nevertheless, this new definition makes tail recursion possible provided that the arguments are evaluated from left to right, which is the normal order. For the computation of the sum of the elements in a list the accumulator should be, of course, initialized to zero. That is, the sum of the elements of x will be computed as the value of

$$((sum)0)x$$

The product of an arbitrary sequence of numbers can be defined in a similar fashion. But, we can also define a generalized function *reduce* to capture the similarities in these definitions. Consider namely, the following definition:

$(((reduce)a)b)x = $ *if* (**null**)x *then* a

$\qquad$ *else* $(((reduce)((b)a)(\wedge)x)b)(\sim)x$

where a is the accumulator parameter and b is a binary operator. This will be written as

$reduce = \lambda a.\lambda b.\lambda x.(((null)x)a)(((reduce)((b)a)(\wedge)x)b)(\sim)x$

and hence,

$sum = ((reduce)0)+$

$prod = ((reduce)1)*$

Both of these functions are well-defined for the empty list, which is quite reasonable in standard mathematics.

In order to get a flavor of list manipulation in our extended lambda-calculus we show a few more examples. We shall use syntactic sugar while omitting the fairly trivial translations to pure lambda-notation.

Examples

The *inner* product of two vectors:

$((inner)x)y = (sum)((map)prod)((pairs)x)y$

where

$((pairs)x)y = $ *if* (**null**)x *then* []

$\qquad$ *else* $((\&)[(\wedge)x,(\wedge)y])((pairs)(\sim)x)(\sim)y$

The *length* of a list:

$(length)x = $ *if* (**null**)x *then* 0 *else* (**succ**)$(length)(\sim)x$

or more concisely

$(length)x = (sum)((map)\lambda z.1)x$

which corresponds to our intuitive way of counting the elements of a list.

The set of subsets (i.e., the *powerset*) of a set:

$(powerset)x = $ *if* (**null**)x *then* [[]]

else ((*append*)(*powerset*)(~)x)((*map*)(&)(∧)x)(*powerset*)(~)x

Here the first argument of *map* is an application of the binary function & to a single argument (∧)x. But this gives a unary function which is fine with *map*. Actually, the function *powerset* works on lists rather than sets. In a list repetitions are permitted and they cannot be filtered out, since the equality problem of λ-expressions is unsolvable in general.

The *last* element of a list:

(*last*)x = *if* (**null**)(~)x *then*(∧)x *else* (*last*)(~)x

The *reverse* of a list:

(*reverse*)x = *if* (**null**)(~)x *then* x *else* ((*append*)(*reverse*)(~)x)[(∧)x]

A sequence of integers from 1 to n:

(*iota*)n = *if* n=1 *then* [1] *else* ((*append*)(*iota*)(**pred**)n)[n]

or equivalently

(*iota*)n = *if* n=1 *then* [1] *else* ((&)1)((*map*)**succ**)(*iota*)(**pred**)n

A sequence of integers from n down to 1:

(*down*)n = *if* n=1 *then* [1] *else* ((&)n)(*down*)(**pred**)n

Sorting of a list of numbers:

(*sort*)x = *if* (**null**)x *then* [] *else* ((*insert*)(∧)x)(*sort*)(~)x

where

((*insert*)a)x = *if* (**null**)x *then* [a]

   else if a≤(∧)x *then* ((&)a)x

   else ((&)(∧)x)((*insert*)a)(~)x

A somewhat tricky example is finding the permutations of a list. We shall use two auxiliary functions. The first will separately remove each element in turn from a list. For instance,

(*removeone*)[a,b,c]

will produce the nested list

[[b,c],[a,c],[a,b]]

This function can be defined as follows

> (*removeone*)x = *if* (**null**)x *then* []
>
> *else* ((&)(~)x)((*map*)(&)(^)x)(*removeone*)(~)x

The next step would be to compute the permutations of those shorter lists which are produced by *removeone*. This we can do by computing

> ((*map*)*permute*)(*removeone*)[a,b,c]

which yields

> ((*map*)*permute*)[[b,c],[a,c],[a,b]]

hence,

> [(*permute*)[b,c],(*permute*)[a,c],(*permute*)[a,b]]

that is,

> [[[b,c],[c,b]], [[a,c],[c,a]], [[a,b],[b,a]]]

provided that *permute* is working correctly. Now, we need another function to put back here the missing elements. That is, we want

> ((*putback*)[a,b,c])[[[b,c],[c,b]],[[a,c],[c,a]],[[a,b],[b,a]]]

to produce the list

> [[a,b,c],[a,c,b],[b,a,c],[b,c,a],[c,a,b],[c,b,a]]

Such a function can be defined this way:

> ((*putback*)x)y = *if* (**null**)x *then* []
>
> *else* ((*append*)((*map*)(&)(^)x)(^)y)((*putback*)(~)x)(~)y

Hence, the permutations can be computed by the function

> (*permute*)x = *if* (**null**)(~)x *then* [x]
>
> *else* ((*putback*)x)((*map*)*permute*)(*removeone*)x

Nested lists can be used, of course, to represent matrices, i.e. *n*-dimensional arrays. The *transposition* of a two-dimensional rectangular array in this representation can be performed by the following function:

$$(transpose)x = if (\textbf{null})(\wedge)x \; then \; []$$

$$else \; ((\&)((map)\wedge)x)(transpose)((map)\sim)x$$

List structures are indeed very useful in many applications. They are considered fundamental in LISP and in other functional languages. It seems natural that they should be treated as primitive objects in λ-calculus, as well, but in order to do so it was necessary to add new reduction rules to the system. By using the γ-rules and a few primitive list operators list manipulation is quite simple in lambda-calculus.

4.4 Dealing with mutual recursion

The use of lists as primitive objects in λ-calculus has some other benefits, too. For one thing, they allow for an effective vectorization of our calculus. This, besides its mathematical elegance, also has some practical advantages as can be seen from the following treatment of mutual recursion. A similar approach has been used by Burge [Burg75] without the full list manipulating power of our extended calculus.

Nonrecursive function definitions can be treated in lambda-calculus in a fairly simple manner. Assume namely, that we have a sequence of definitions of the form

$$f_1 = e_1$$
.
.
.
$$f_n = e_n$$

where f_i are variables (function names) and e_i are λ-expressions. Assume further, that E is a λ-expession containing free occurrences of the variables

f_i (i = 1,...,n). Now, the value of E with respect to the given definitions can be computed by evaluating the combined expression

$$(\lambda f_1 \ ... \ (\lambda f_n E)e_n...)e_1$$

Thus, the set of equations can be treated as mere syntactic sugar having a trivial translation into pure lambda-notation. This simple-minded approach, however, does not always work. As can be seen from the given translation, the form of the combined expression reflects the order of the equations. Therefore, a free occurrence of f_i in e_j will be replaced by e_i if and only if i<j.

In other words, *previously defined function names can be used on the right-hand sides of the equations, but no forward reference can be made to a function name defined only later in the sequence.* This clearly excludes mutual recursion, which always involves some forward reference. If, for instance, f_1 is defined in terms of f_2 (i.e., f_2 occurs in e_1) and vice versa then the forward reference cannot be eliminated simply by changing the order of the equations.

It should be clear that in the absence of mutual recursion the equations can be rearranged in such a way that no forward reference occurs. Immediate recursion should not be a problem, because it can be resolved with the aid of the **Y** combinator. Now, we will show that mutual recursion can be resolved fairly easily in our extended lambda-calculus. In particular, the list manipulating power of our calculus is very helpful in working with a list of variables. Actually, *we can use a single variable to represent a list* just as is done in vector algebra. Hence, the solution of a set of simultaneous equations can be expressed in a compact form with a single occurrence of the **Y** combinator. First, we illustrate this method through an example.

Consider the following mutual recursion defining two number-theoretic (integer type) functions, g and h:

$(g)n = $ *if* $(\mathbf{zero})n$ *then* 0 *else* $((+)(g)(\mathbf{pred})n)(h)(\mathbf{pred})n$

$(h)n = $ *if* $(\mathbf{zero})n$ *then* 1 *else* $((*)(g)n)(h)(\mathbf{pred})n$

In our 'sugar free' λ-notation these are written as

$g = \lambda n.(((\mathbf{zero})n)0)((+)(g)(\mathbf{pred})n)(h)(\mathbf{pred})n$

$h = \lambda n.(((\mathbf{zero})n)1)((*)(g)n)(h)(\mathbf{pred})n$

We introduce a new variable F to represent the ordered pair [g,h], and re-write our equations using (1)F instead of g, and (2)F instead of h.

(1)F = λn.(((**zero**)n)0)((+)((1)F)(**pred**)n((2)F)(**pred**)n

(2)F = λn.(((**zero**)n)1)((*)((1)F)n)((2)F)(**pred**)n

By combining the two equations we get

F = [λn.(((**zero**)n)0)((+)((1)F)(**pred**)n)((2)F)(**pred**)n,

   λn.(((**zero**)n)1)((*)((1)F)n)((2)F)(**pred**)n]

Abstracting with respect to F on the right-hand side yields the following fixed point equation:

F = (λf.[λn.(((**zero**)n)0)((+)((1)f)(**pred**)n)((2)f)(**pred**)n,

   λn.(((**zero**)n)1)((*)((1)f)n)((2)f)(**pred**)n])F

whose solution is given by

F = (Y)λf.[λn.(((**zero**)n)0)((+)((1)f)(**pred**)n)((2)f)(**pred**)n,

   λn(((**zero**)n)1)((*)((1)f)n)((2)f)(**pred**)n]

This solution can be used to compute, for example, the value of (F)3, which is the same as [(g)3, (h)3]. The computation can be performed by using our reduction rules only.

The same technique can be used in general for any set of simultaneous recursion equations

$f_1 = e_1$

.

.

.

$f_n = e_n$

First we rewrite each e_k by substituting (i)F for the free occurrences of f_i $(1 \leq i \leq n)$. The resulting expressions will be denoted by R_k which form an ordered n-tuple

$[R_1, ..., R_n]$

So, we get the defining equation

$F = [R_1, ..., R_n]$

in place of the original ones. Abstracting with respect to F on the right-hand side yields

$F = (\lambda f.[r_1, ..., r_n])F$

where each r_i is obtained from R_i (i=1, ..., n) by substituting f for F. The solution of this fixed-point equation is expressed by

$F = (Y)\lambda f.[r_1, ..., r_n]$

In order to prove that this is a correct solution we apply our reduction rules. The right-hand side of the last equation reduces to

$(\lambda f.[r_1, ..., r_n])(Y)\lambda f.[r_1, ..., r_n]$

by the definition of the Y combinator. This further reduces to

$([\lambda f.r_1, ..., \lambda f.r_n])(Y)\lambda f.[r_1, ..., r_n]$

by $\gamma 2$, and then to

$[(\lambda f.r_1)(Y)\lambda f.[r_1, ..., r_n], ... , (\lambda f.r_n)(Y)\lambda f.[r_1, ..., r_n]]$

by $\gamma 1$. This is clearly an n-tuple which should be equal to F. Indeed, its i-th component is

$(\lambda f.r_i)(Y)\lambda f.[r_1, ..., r_n]$

which implies that

$(\lambda f.r_i)F = R_i$

provided that F satisfies the equation

$F = [R_1, ..., R_n]$

and this completes the proof.

Now, the value of any λ-expression E with respect to the given recursive definitions is computed as the value of the combined expression

$(\lambda F.G)(Y)\lambda f.[r_1, ..., r_n]$

where

$G = (\lambda f_1 ... (\lambda f_n.E)(n)F ...)(1)F$

This formula is correct also for nonrecursive definitions but, of course, the simple-minded approach described at the beginning of this section is more efficient. Therefore, an optimizing compiler should treat recursive and non recursive definitions separately. For that purpose, one can compute the dependency relation between the given definitions and check if it forms a partial order on the set functions f_i ($i = 1, ..., n$). If so, then no mutual recursion is present and the definitions can be arranged in a sequence suitable for the simple-minded solution. Otherwise, one should try to iso-late the minimal sets of mutually recursive definitions and solve them sep-arately, before putting them back to their proper place in the sequence.

4.5 Computing with infinite lists

Infinite lists occur in a natural way as the output of nonterminating com-putations. Such computations are not necessarily wrong but, of course, they would sooner or later run out of time and/or space. Nevertheless, their finite initial portion may contain valuable information and in many cases an a priori upper bound on their lengths seems rather artificial. For instance, we may want to write a program to generate a sequence of natural numbers, square numbers, or prime numbers, without limiting the length of the list in advance. Such open ended lists are relatively easy to generate, but it is far more difficult to use them as intermediate results.

The difficulty arises when we try to pass a potentially infinite list as an argument to a function. The application of the function cannot be de-layed until the entire list is computed, because it may take an infinite amount of time. But how many elements are actually needed for the com-putation of the function? The answer depends on the function itself and there is no general rule. For instance, the special function **null** needs only the first element to see that the list is not empty. Similarly, the ∧ and the ~ functions can be computed as soon as the first element appears. On the other hand, the *sum* of an infinite sequence can never be totally computed, but we may compute partial sums to approximate the result. So, we may consider partial application of certain functions, which is related to the idea of tail recursion. (See the discussion of the continued arithmetic operations in Section 4.3.)

The best way to deal with potentially infinite lists is to follow a so called demand-driven evaluation strategy. This means that we compute only as much of an argument as is indeed necessary for the computation of the given function. This also implies that the order of the evaluation should be top-down, or outside-in, so that the function is examined first, before any of its arguments is evaluated. This clearly corresponds to the normal order evaluation in standard lambda-calculus. But here we have some new problems due to the presence of special functions and their specific reduction rules.

The power of demand-driven evaluation may be characterized by the fact that it allows for non-strict functions. A function is called non-strict if its value is well-defined for some undefined arguments. For instance, the conditional expression

if A *then* B *else* C

is considered non-strict in its second and third arguments, because B need not be evaluated when A happens to be false, and C need not be evaluated in the opposite case. Therefore, B or C may occasionally be undefined without making the whole expression undefined.

For another example, the operation of multiplication may be defined as a semi-strict function, i.e. non-strict in its second argument. All we have to do is to compute the first argument first, and check if it is zero. If it is not zero then we have to evaluate the second argument, as well. However, if it is zero, we can return the value zero as a result regardless of the second operand. Thus, the second argument may be undefined (involving a non-terminating computation) while the function is still well-defined.

Even if an argument is actually used for the computation of the value of a function, it may not have to be fully evaluated for that purpose. Therefore, the evaluation of an argument should be suspended as soon as possible, that is, when the partially evaluated argument is sufficient for the computation of the function.

Now, let us see how to compute infinite lists in our extended lambda-calculus. Take, for instance, an infinite list of zeros. We can define this list recursively as follows:

zeros = ((&)0)*zeros*

which means that the infinite list of zeros remains the same when one more
zero is attached to it. But this is a fixed-point equation whose solution is

$$zeros = (\mathbf{Y})\lambda z.((\&)0)z$$

Indeed, the right-hand side reduces to

$$(\lambda z.((\&)0)z)(\mathbf{Y})\lambda z.((\&)0)z$$

and then to

$$((\&)0)(\mathbf{Y})\lambda z.((\&)0)z$$

which clearly generates an infinite list of zeros just by using the given reduction rules. Unfortunately, the form in which this list appears is not
suitable for using it as an argument to our 'built-in' functions. For instance,
the special function $\wedge$ cannot work on this list, because it does not have the
appropriate form. But, this is easy to fix. All we have to is to adjust the
reduction rules of the list operators to make them work with partially
evaluated lists. So, the rest of a list may be an arbitrary λ-expression which
has not been computed yet. This implies, of course, that the rest of the list,
which will be denoted by R in the following rules, may not reduce to a
'list-tail' or may not have a normal form at all. Nevertheless, we can define
our list operators as follows:

$$((\&)E)R \rightarrow [E, R$$

$$(\mathbf{null})[E, R \rightarrow \mathbf{false}$$

$$(\wedge)[E, R \rightarrow E$$

$$(\sim)[E, R \rightarrow R$$

$$(1)[E, R \rightarrow E$$

$$(k)[E, R \rightarrow ((\mathbf{pred})k)R \qquad \text{for } k>1$$

These rules represent the *lazy* extensions of the defining rules of the given
functions. With the aid of these rules we can easily compute, for example,
$(5)zeros$, which is the fifth member of the infinite list, that is, 0.

   The infinite list of natural numbers is defined by the iteration of the
successor function. The iteration of a function f to some argument x
generates the infinite list

[x, (f)x, (f)(f)x, ...]

which can be defined recursively as

$$((iterate)f)x = ((\&)x)((iterate)f)(f)x$$

The explicit form of this function is given by

$$iterate = (Y)\lambda i.\lambda f.\lambda x.((\&)x)((i)f)(f)x$$

So, the infinite sequence of natural numbers is

$$numbers = ((iterate)\mathbf{succ})0$$

A more interesting example is the list of Fibonacci numbers

[1, 1, 2, 3, 5, 8, 13, ...]

where each element is the sum of the previous two. An auxiliary function can be used, which builds such a sequence from two arbitrary initial values.

$$((build)x)y := ((\&)x)((build)y)((+)x)y$$

Hence,

$$build = (Y)\lambda b.\lambda x.\lambda y.((\&)x)((b)y)((+)x)y$$

and

$$fibonacci = ((build)1)1$$

Another way of defining the *fibonacci* list is based on the following observation. By adding together the corresponding elements of two Fibonacci sequences with the first sequence being offset by one, we get the tail of the same Fibonacci sequence as a result. That is,

$$[1, 1, 2, 3, \ 5, \ 8, \ 13, ...]$$

$$+ [1, 1, 2, 3, 5, \ 8, 13, \ 21, ...]$$

$$= [1, 2, 3, 5, 8, 13, 21, 34, ...]$$

This is used in the following definition:

$$fibonacci = ((append)[1,1])((map)sum)((pairs)fibonacci)(\sim)fibonacci$$

where

$$((pairs)x)y = ((\&)[(\wedge)x, (\wedge)y])((pairs)(\sim)x)(\sim)y$$

Note that in the definition of pairs we do not have to test for the empty list, since neither *fibonacci* nor $(\sim)$*fibonacci* is empty. An interesting feature of this definition is the application of *(map)sum* to an infinite list of pairs. Clearly, this application should not wait for the computation of the whole list. As soon as the first pair gets formed by the function *pairs*, its *sum* should be computed and appended to the list [1, 1]. This yields an intermediate result whose first three elements are 1, 1, 2, and thus, the computation of *pairs* may continue. This method of building the infinite list of Fibonacci numbers works only with a demand-driven evaluation strategy. Otherwise, the application of the functions would be delayed until the arguments are totally computed, which would obviously kill the recursion in this case. This is so, because the list *fibonacci* is used here repeatedly as a partially evaluated argument while it is being created.

It is important to note that we do not have to take extra measures in order to deal with infinite lists. The demand-driven evaluation technique as described above will automatically give us this opportunity for free. Later we shall see that a strictly demand-driven evaluation technique usually involves some loss in the efficiency of computations. Therefore, the overall simplicity of handling infinite lists does have a price.

For another example with this flavor, consider the computation of the prime numbers using the Sieve of Eratosthenes. First, an auxiliary function is defined to filter out the multiples of a number from a list of numbers.

$$((filter)n)x = if \text{ (\textbf{null})}x \text{ then } []$$

$$else \text{ } if((\textbf{mod})(\wedge)x)n = 0 \text{ then } ((filter)n)(\sim)x$$

$$else \text{ } ((\&)(\wedge)x)((filter)n)(\sim)x$$

The **mod** function is one of our primitive functions defined on integers. It gives the remainder of the division of its first argument by its second argument. Now, *sieve* will be defined as

$$(sieve)x = ((\&)(\wedge)x)(sieve)((filter)(\wedge)x)(\sim)x$$

and hence, the infinite list of prime numbers is computed by

$$primes = (sieve)((iterate)\textbf{succ})2$$

Observe again that *sieve* can be computed only in a demand-driven fashion. Actually, the boundaries between the computation of a function and the computation of its argument(s) are completely blurred by demand-driven evaluation.

Infinite lists are also useful for approximations in numerical analysis. Take, for example, the evaluation of the exponential function using its Taylor series. The rest of the infinite series starting with the (n-1)-st term is

$$t_{n-1} + t_n + \dots$$

where

$$t_n = t_{n-1}\frac{x}{n}$$

Hence, it can be defined recursively as

$$rest = \lambda t.\lambda n.\lambda x.((\&)t)(((rest)((*)t)((/)x)n)(\text{succ})n)x$$

Now, if we want to stop at the first such term that is smaller than a given ε then we can write

$$rest = \lambda t.\lambda\varepsilon.\lambda n.\lambda x.((((<)t)\varepsilon)[])((\&)t)((((rest)((*)t)((/)x)n)\varepsilon)(\text{succ})n)x$$

Hence, the approximate value of the exponential function e^x for $x > 0$ can be computed by

$$exp = \lambda x.(sum)((((rest)1)\varepsilon)1)x$$

As can be seen from these examples infinite lists can be defined easily via recursion. Infinite objects and, in particular, infinite lists occur naturally in mathematics but they are poorly represented in conventional programming languages, because their proper treatment requires lazy evaluation which seems to be less efficient than the traditional approach. Clearly, there is a trade-off between the expressive power of the language and the efficiency of its implementation.

Another problem here, and also in most functional languages including LISP, is the lack of distinction between fixed-sized arrays and dynamically changeable lists. The fixed size of a finite array makes it easy for an implementation to support a direct access to its elements. List structures are more flexible, hence, a direct access to their elements is much more difficult to obtain. A uniform treatment of arrays and lists must be prepared for the

worst case which makes it less efficient. Therefore, it seems desirable to
introduce separate data structures for arrays and lists, and use arrays rather
than lists whenever possible.

Sequential input and output files can be treated naturally as infinite
lists. They are often called *streams* in this context and they are evaluated
lazily just like any other infinite objects. One must be careful, however,
with their implementation to avoid side effects.

Exercises

4.1 Define list manipulating functions to do the following:

(a) Sort a list of numbers using *quicksort*,

(b) Merge, i.e. shuffle two lists,

(c) Cut off the last element of a list,

(d) Rotate a list to the right or to the left,

(e) Compare the elements of two lists,

(f) Multiply together two square matrices.

4.2 A *Curried* function with precisely n arguments will be changed into the
corresponding list oriented function (which takes a list of lenght n for an
argument) by the following combinator

uncurry =

$$\lambda n.\lambda g.\lambda v.(((\textbf{zero})(\textbf{pred})n)(g)(1)v)((((\textit{uncurry})(\textbf{pred})n)g)v)(n)v$$

So, for instance, with n = 3 we get

$$(((\textit{uncurry})3)F)[a,b,c] = (((F)a)b)c$$

Conversely, a function whose argument is an array (list) of n elements will
be changed into the corresponding *Curried* function by the following
combinator:

$$\textit{curry} = \lambda n.\lambda f.(((\textbf{zero})(\textbf{pred})n)\lambda x.(f)[x])$$

$$((\textit{curry})(\textbf{pred})n)\lambda w.\lambda x.(f)((\textit{append})w)[x]$$

Use these combinators to

(a) unCurry the function *gcd* of Exercise 3.8,

(b) Curry a list oriented function defined on ordered triples,

(c) prove that each of the above two combinators is an inverse of the other.

4.3 Are these two function definitions equivalent?

$diff = \lambda x.(((\textbf{null})x)0)((-)(1)x)(diff)(\sim)x$

$diff = \lambda x.(((\textbf{null})x)0)(((\textbf{null})(\sim)x)(1)x)(diff)((\&)((-)(1)x)(2)x)(\sim)(\sim)x$

CHAPTER FIVE

RULE-BASED SEMANTICS OF λ-EXPRESSIONS

5.1 Program transformation as a computation

The semantics of a language *L* can be defined in general as a mapping μ from *L* to *M*, where *M* is the set of 'meanings'. For the sake of simplicity, the elements of *L* will be called *syntactic objects* while the elements of *M* will be called *semantic objects*. Our syntactic objects are the λ-expressions which form a context-free language to be denoted by Λ. Thus, for every λ-expression E ϵ Λ its meaning will be defined as the value of $\mu(E)$ ϵ *M*.

So far, we have defined only Λ but we have not specified the set *M*. In order to have a formal definition we need some symbolic representation for the elements of *M*, that is, we need a notational system (a language) also for *M*. Moreover, we must have an intimate knowledge of the semantic objects belonging in *M*, otherwise they would not help us understand Λ.

The language we know best is, of course, our native tongue, but the spoken languages do not have the mathematical precision we need. A precise mathematical notation would be the ideal thing. We all agree, for example, on the meaning of an integer in decimal notation. We can also rely upon the decimal notation for representing rational numbers and, by allowing infinite sequences, real numbers, as well. For a reasonable representation of the meaning of more complex λ-expressions we need, of course, more complex semantical objects. The question is what kinds of mathematical objects are needed for the definition of the meaning of arbitrary λ-expressions, and how to denote those objects.

What if we choose a well-defined subset $\Lambda_0 \subseteq \Lambda$ for the language M? This may sound strange (circular) at first, but it makes a lot of sense. Numbers, for one thing, are represented here in decimal notation which is no different from their representation in standard mathematics. The same is true for other constants and variables. So, we do not have to worry about those primitive objects and thus, we can concentrate on the representation of functions and other more complex structures. The question is what other specific constructs from Λ are to be used for a reasonable semantical description of the entire Λ. We want to define the meaning of λ-expressions in terms of those special kinds of λ-expressions whose meaning is (assumed to be) self-evident. The mapping μ would then assign a member of this subset Λ_0 to every expression in Λ.

For any definition of μ *the meaning must be invariant under β-equality.* Therefore, the simplest solution in this regard is to choose **the set of λ-expressions being in normal form** for $M = \Lambda_0 \subseteq \Lambda$, and define the mapping μ as **reducing to normal form**.

A summary of the reduction rules which form the basis of this definition will be given below. There is, however, a serious problem with this definition of μ, since it is a partial rather than a total function on Λ and, unfortunately, *there are many intuitively meaningful λ-expressions without normal form.* The most important ones are the recursive definitions involving the **Y** combinator giving rise to an infinite reduction sequence. In spite of that, the simplicity of this approach makes it worth studying. As a matter of fact, *Church himself regarded λ-expressions without normal form as meaningless.*

For the sake of completeness we also summarize here the syntax of the language Λ.

THE SYNTAX OF λ-EXPRESSIONS:

<λ-expression>::=<variable> | <constant> | <abstraction> |

<application> | <list>

<variable>::=<identifier>

<constant>::=<number> | <operator> | <combinator>

<abstraction>::= λ<variable>.<λ-expression>

<application>::= (<λ-expression>)<λ-expression>

<list>::= [<λ-expression><list-tail> | []

<list-tail>::= ,<λ-expression><list-tail> |]

<operator>::=<arithmetic operator> | <relational operator> |

   <predicate> | <boolean operator> | <list operator>

<arithmetic operator>::= + | − | * | / | **succ** | **pred** | **mod**

<relational operator>::=< | ≤ | = | ≥ | > | ≠

<predicate>::= **zero** | **null**

<boolean operator>::= **and** | **or** | **not**

<list operator>::= ∧ | ~ | & | **map** | **append**

<combinator>::= **true** | **false** | **Y**

This syntax does not specify what an identifier or a number looks like, but any reasonable definition would do, and we are not interested in their details. What we are interested in right now is the meaning of λ-expressions which will be described with the aid of a set of reduction rules.

These reduction rules represent *meaning preserving* transformations on λ-expressions and the corresponding equality (in the sense of Definition 2.6) divides Λ into *equivalence classes* each of which consists of λ-expressions with the same meaning. If an equivalence class contains a member from Λ_0 then this member is unique up to α-congruence and it represents the meaning of every λ-expression in that class. The following is a summary of our reduction rules.

ALPHA RULES

(α1)   {z/x}x → z

(α2) $\{z/x\}E \rightarrow E$ if x does not occur free in E

(α3) $\{z/x\}\lambda y.E \rightarrow \lambda y.\{z/x\}E$ for every λ-expression E, if $x \not\equiv y \not\equiv z$.

(α4) $\{z/x\}(E_1)E_2 \rightarrow (\{z/x\}E_1)\{z/x\}E_2$

(α5) $\{z/x\}[E_1,...,E_n] \rightarrow [\{z/x\}E_1,..., \{z/x\}E_n]$ for $n \geq 0$

BETA RULES

(β1) $(\lambda x.x)Q \rightarrow Q$

(β2) $(\lambda x.E)Q \rightarrow E$ if x does not occur free in E

(β3) $(\lambda x.\lambda y.E)Q \rightarrow \lambda z.(\lambda x.\{z/y\}E)Q$ if $x \not\equiv y$, and z is neither free
                                                    nor bound in (E)Q

(β4) $(\lambda x.(E_1)E_2)Q \rightarrow ((\lambda x.E_1)Q)(\lambda x.E_2)Q$

GAMMA RULES

(γ1) $([E_1, ..., E_n])Q \rightarrow [(E_1)Q, ..., E_n)Q]$ for $n \geq 0$

(γ2) $\lambda x.[E_1, ..., E_n] \rightarrow [\lambda x.E_1, ..., \lambda x.E_n]$ for $n \geq 0$

LIST MANIPULATING FUNCTIONS

$(\wedge)[] \rightarrow []$, $(\wedge)[E_1,E_2...,E_n] \rightarrow E_1$

$(\sim)[] \rightarrow []$, $(\sim)[E_1,E_2,...,E_n] \rightarrow [E_2,...,E_n]$

$((\&)A)[] \rightarrow [A]$, $((\&)A)[E_1,...,E_n] \rightarrow [A, E_1,...,E_n]$

$(\textbf{null})[] \rightarrow \textbf{true}$, $(\textbf{null})[E_1,...,E_n] \rightarrow \textbf{false}$ for $n \geq 1$

$((\textbf{map})F)[] \rightarrow []$, $((\textbf{map})F)[E_1,...,E_n] \rightarrow [(F)E_1,...,(F)E_n]$

$((\textbf{append})[])[E_1,...,E_n] \rightarrow [E_1,...,E_n]$

$((\textbf{append})[A_1,...,A_m])[E_1,...,E_n] \rightarrow [A_1,...,A_m, E_1,...,E_n]$

PROJECTIONS

$(1)[E_1, ..., E_n] \rightarrow E_1$ for $n \geq 1$

$$(k)[E_1, ..., E_n] \rightarrow ((\textbf{pred})k)[E_2, ..., E_n] \quad \text{for } k \geq 2, n \geq 1.$$

COMBINATORS

$$((\textbf{true})A)B \rightarrow A, \qquad\qquad ((\textbf{false})A)B \rightarrow B$$

$$(\textbf{Y})E \rightarrow (E)(\textbf{Y})E$$

OPERATORS AND PREDICATES

$((\textbf{and})\textbf{true})\textbf{true} \rightarrow \textbf{true}$ $\qquad ((\textbf{and})\textbf{true})\textbf{false} \rightarrow \textbf{false}$

$((\textbf{and})\textbf{false})\textbf{true} \rightarrow \textbf{false}$ $\qquad ((\textbf{and})\textbf{false})\textbf{false} \rightarrow \textbf{false}$

$((\textbf{or})\textbf{true})\textbf{true} \rightarrow \textbf{true}$ $\qquad ((\textbf{or})\textbf{true})\textbf{false} \rightarrow \textbf{true}$

$((\textbf{or})\textbf{false})\textbf{true} \rightarrow \textbf{true}$ $\qquad ((\textbf{or})\textbf{false})\textbf{false} \rightarrow \textbf{false}$

$(\textbf{not})\textbf{true} \rightarrow \textbf{false}$ $\qquad (\textbf{not})\textbf{false} \rightarrow \textbf{true}$

$(\textbf{zero})0 \rightarrow \textbf{true}$ $\qquad (\textbf{zero})n \rightarrow \textbf{false} \quad \text{for } n \neq 0$

$((+)m)n \rightarrow k \quad$ if m,n,k are numbers and $k = m + n$

$((-)m)n \rightarrow k \quad$ if m,n,k are numbers and $k = m - n$

$((*)m)n \rightarrow k \quad$ if m,n,k are numbers and $k = m * n$

$((/)m)n \rightarrow k \quad$ if m,n,k are numbers and $k = m + n$

$((\textbf{mod})m)n \rightarrow k \quad$ if m,n,k are numbers and $k = m \textbf{ mod } n$

$(\textbf{succ})m \rightarrow n \quad$ if m,n are integers and $n = m + 1$

$(\textbf{pred})m \rightarrow n \quad$ if m,n are integers, $m > 0$, and $n = m - 1$

$((<)m)n \rightarrow \textbf{true} \quad$ if m,n are numbers and $m < n$

$((<)m)n \rightarrow \textbf{false} \quad$ if m,n are numbers and $m \geq n$

Similar reduction rules are used for the remaining relational operators and this completes our list.

Note that most of the above rules are, in fact, 'rule-schemas' rather than individual rules as they have an infinite number of instances. *The evaluation of a λ-expression will be performed by reducing it to its normal form using the above rules.* But this is the same as the execution of the algorithm (or functional program) represented by the expression. So, the execution of a program can be described as a sequence of reduction steps where each step is a single application of some reduction rule. This means that the execution of a program can be defined in terms of certain transformations performed directly on its source form. Actually, the program and its result are considered here as two equivalent representations of the same object.

According to the Church–Rosser Theorem, the order in which the reduction steps are performed does not matter provided that the reduction process terminates after a finite number of steps. From a practical point of view, however, it would be desirable to minimize the number of steps that are needed for the evaluation of a λ-expression. That is essentially the same as minimizing the execution time of a functional program, which cannot be done in general. Nevertheless, there are various techniques for improving the run-time efficiency of a program. The efficiency of the function evaluation process represents a major issue for the implementation techniques to be studied in Chapters 6 and 7.

This reduction-based approach to the semantics of λ-expresions is closely related to the so called *'operational semantics'* of programs. Indeed, the reduction process is a well-defined procedure for every λ-expression even if it does not terminate. It is nondeterministic though in the sense that the redex to be contracted in each step may be chosen arbitrarily from among those that are present in the given λ-expression at that point.

5.2 Controlled reduction

In Section 5.1 we identified the meaning of a λ-expression with its normal form. This definition of the meaning is clearly not satisfactory since two important questions remain to be answered:

1. What to do with λ-expressions without normal forms?

2. What to do with λ-expression whose normal forms have no self-evident meanings?

If every λ-expression without normal form is considered meaningless then *we are faced with the awkward situation of having meaningful λ-expressions containing meaningless subexpressions.* Indeed, a λ-expression involving the **Y** combinator may represent a recursive function without having normal form. But, when it is applied to some other λ-expression(s) then the resulting expression may have a normal form which represents the value of the given function. Thus, the value of the function may be well-defined for at least some argument(s) without the meaning of the function itself being defined.

To avoid this conflict we propose the following compromise. We introduce the notion of *controlled reduction*, which is defined by the following adjustments to the reduction rules:

The rule for the **Y** *combinator will be changed to*

$$(\mathbf{Y'})E \rightarrow (E)(\mathbf{Y})E$$

where **Y'** *is a newly introduced combinator. Furthermore, the β2-rule will be modified as*

(β2')   (λx.E)Q → E' *if x does not occur free in* E,

where E' *is the same as* E *except that each (if any) occurrence of* **Y** *in* E *is replaced by* **Y'**.

In order for the new system to work, all recursive definitions should be written with the aid of the new **Y'** combinator in place of the original **Y**. The latter is disabled in the new system until it gets changed to **Y'** in a β2'-reduction step.

To see how this system works on a simple example consider the following recursive definition of the factorial function.

$$(\text{fact})n = if\ n = 0\ then\ 1\ else\ ((*)n)(\text{fact})(\mathbf{pred})n$$

which will be written in our λ-notation as

$$(\text{fact})n = (((\mathbf{zero})n)1)((*)n)(\text{fact})(\mathbf{pred})n$$

that is

$$\text{fact} = \lambda n.(((\mathbf{zero})n)1)((*)n)(\text{fact})(\mathbf{pred})n$$

The solution of this recursion equation will be expressed by

$$\text{fact} = (\mathbf{Y'})\lambda f.\lambda n.(((\mathbf{zero})n)1)((*)n)(f)(\mathbf{pred})n$$

where the right-hand side reduces to the normal form

$$\lambda n.(((\mathbf{zero})n)1)((*)n)((\mathbf{Y})\lambda f.\lambda n.(((\mathbf{zero})n)1)((*)n)(f)(\mathbf{pred})n) \;(\mathbf{pred})n$$

If, however, we supply an argument, say 5, to the function fact then we get the correct result 120 as can be easily checked by the reader.

The trick of *controlled reduction* lies in the fact that the $\mathbf{Y'}$ combinator can fire only once, but each time an argument Q is presented to an expression of the form

$$(F)(Y)F$$

an attempt at evaluating the expression

$$((F)(Y)F)Q$$

is made, which in turn involves an attempt at substituting the argument Q for some variable in $\mathbf{Y}$. But that would change $\mathbf{Y}$ to $\mathbf{Y'}$, since no variable occurs free in $\mathbf{Y}$.

It is necessary, however, that the expression F has at least one more abstraction besides the abstraction on the function name that is being defined by the recursion. This is the case in the above example where we have λn besides the λf. Indeed, any well-founded recursion must have a condition which would terminate the recursion after a finite number of steps. That condition must depend on the argument(s), otherwise there could be no change in its truth value throughout the recursion.

It is interesting to note that this modified system is not extensional since we have

$$(\lambda x.\mathbf{Y'})Q = (\lambda x.\mathbf{Y})Q \quad \text{for any } Q,$$

which would imply $\lambda x.\mathbf{Y'} = \lambda x.\mathbf{Y}$ in an extensionally complete system. (Actually, we may assume that this is the case even though $\mathbf{Y'} \neq \mathbf{Y}$.)

In any case, *the meaning function μ can be defined as reducing to normal form in the new system*. If the normal form of an expression has a subexpression of the form $(\mathbf{Y})F$ then this subexpression denotes the fixed-point of F.

Note that the $\mathbf{Y}$ combinator can also be used for defining infinite lists. For instance, an infinite list of zeros can be defined recursively as zeros = ((&)0)zeros

hence,

zeros = $(\mathbf{Y'})\lambda z.((\&)0)z$

where the right-hand side reduces to

$(\lambda z.((\&)0)z)(\mathbf{Y})\lambda z.((\&)0)z$

which has the normal form

$((\&)0)(\mathbf{Y})\lambda z.((\&)0)z$

Now, the problem is that a finite projection of this infinite list is not computable in the new system.

First of all, we have to define all list operations in a *lazy* manner as discussed in Section 4.5. So, for example, the k-th element of an infinite list will be obtained by extending the reduction rules of projections to infinite lists as follows:

$(1)[E_1, ...] \rightarrow E_1$

$(k)[E_1, ...] \rightarrow ((\mathbf{pred})k)[E_2, ...]$

All the other list manipulating functions, which are the $\wedge$, $\sim$, &, **null**, **map**, and **append**, will also be defined *lazily*. Actually, the last two need not be defined as primitives, since they can be defined recursively with the aid of the others as shown in Section 4.3. Namely,

$((\mathbf{map})f)x = (((\mathbf{null})x)[])((\&)(f)(\wedge)x)((\mathbf{map})f)(\sim)x$

$((\mathbf{append})x)y = (((\mathbf{null})x)y)((\&)(\wedge)x)((\mathbf{append})(\sim)x)y$

Returning to our example, the computation of the k-th element of the infinite list of zeros begins with

$(k)((\&)0)(\mathbf{Y})\lambda z.((\&)0)z \Rightarrow ((\mathbf{pred})k)(\mathbf{Y})\lambda z.((\&)0)z$

when $k \geq 2$. Now, in order to continue this computation we have to change the **Y** combinator back to $\mathbf{Y'}$. But that requires further modifications of the reduction rules, because the $\beta 2'$-rule is not applicable in this case, since the recursively defined infinite list involving the **Y** combinator is not the operator but the operand of the given projection. Therefore, we introduce the following new rules:

$(k)(\mathbf{Y})E \rightarrow (k)(\mathbf{Y'})E$ for $k \geq 1$

$(\wedge)(\mathbf{Y})E \rightarrow (\wedge)(\mathbf{Y'})E$

$(\sim)(\mathbf{Y})E \rightarrow (\sim)(\mathbf{Y'})E$

$(\mathbf{null})(\mathbf{Y})E \rightarrow (\mathbf{null})(\mathbf{Y'})E$

Recursively defined infinite lists can thus be used as arguments in these operations and each time the operator bounces into the **Y** combinator it will change it back to **Y'**.

This system appears to be very helpful for program debugging, as it can catch many errors which would otherwise result in infinite computations. It is, of course, impossible to detect in general whether or not a program would terminate for a given input, because that is equivalent to the halting problem. In particular, it is essential for our technique that the **Y** combinator is represented by a specific token. If it is replaced, for instance, by the λ-expression

$$\lambda y.(\lambda x.(y)(x)x)\lambda x.(y)(x)x$$

then our method would not work.

As regards the second question mentioned at the beginning of this section, the answer is much more difficult. Every λ-expression represents, in fact, a mapping of Λ into itself, since application is defined for all λ-expressions. Therefore, every member of M should also represent a mapping of M to itself. A naïve interpretation of type-free lambda-calculus would also require that every type $[M \rightarrow M]$ mapping be represented by some λ-expression, i.e. by some member of M. (Note that the value of a free variable may range over the entire domain M and thus, the set of all possible meanings of λ-expressions depends not only on Λ but also on M.) However, the cardinality of the set of all $[M \rightarrow M]$ type mappings is always greater than that of M for any nontrivial M.

So, it should not be surprising that it was very difficult to find a satisfactory set-theoretical interpretation of type-free lambda-calculus. The first set-theoretical (or rather lattice-theoretical) model for type-free lambda-calculus was constructed by Dana Scott while he was trying to prove the non-existence of such models.

The main idea behind his construction is the restriction of the model to *Scott-continuous functions*. Continuity in any topology imposes severe restrictions on the behavior of the functions. Therefore, the set of continuous functions is usually much smaller than that of arbitrary functions. In fact, *it is enough to define the value of a continuous function on a sufficiently large (and dense) subset of its domain from which the remaining values will follow*. Hence, the cardinality of the set of *continuous mappings* of *M* to itself is usually much smaller than that of the set of arbitrary mappings with the same type. Moreover, one can find certain domains which have the same cardinality as the set of their continuous mappings to themselves.

Such models are widely used in *Denotational Semantics* where the function μ is defined directly for all syntactic objects. Of course, the meaning of λ-expressions must still be invariant under β-equality, and the difficulty of the proof of this invariance largely depends on the definition of μ. A systematic study of Denotational Semantics goes beyond the scope of this book, but many fine books on this subject are available in the literature.

5.3 The functional programming system FP

In the preceding two sections we defined the semantics of λ-expressions in terms of rewriting rules. The semantics of programming languages can now be defined by translating them to Λ. This can be done, at least theoretically, for every programming language but it is fairly complicated when dealing with conventional (imperative) programming languages. The problem is caused mainly by the use of assignment statements. The value of an expression depends on the values of its variables, which in turn depend on the corresponding assignment statements. Hence, the value of an expression depends on the order of the execution of those assignment statements. In other words, the evaluation of the expressions of a conventional programming language is 'history sensitive', which makes their semantics more complicated.

> *In pure functional languages there are no assignment statements, and the order of the execution of the operations occurring in some expression is restricted only by their partial order defined implicitly by the structure of the given expression.*

This implicit partial order is due to the data-dependencies of the operations. For example, the addition obviously precedes the multiplication in the expression (a+b)*c-d while they can be performed in any order in (a+b)-(c*d). The subtraction is, of course, the last operation in either case.

The foundations of a mathematical theory of functional programming were laid down by John Backus in his Turing Award paper [Back78]. He developed a functional programming system called FP.

> *An* FP *program is simply an expression representing a function that maps objects to objects.*

This means that only first order functions are used in FP which is a significant difference between type-free lambda-calculus and FP. Another more formal difference is the lack of object variables in FP. Each function in FP has only one argument which is not mentioned explicitly in the notation. There is, however, an obvious similarity between the theory of combinators and the variable-free approach to *function level reasoning* advocated by Backus.

A fixed set of program forming operations, called *functional forms* or *combining forms* are used in FP to form new functions from given ones. (These are, in fact, second order functions which take functions as arguments and return functions as results.) A formal description of the FP system is given below.

Given a set of *atoms, THE SET OF OBJECTS O* is defined recursively as follows.

(a) Every *atom* is in *O*.

(b) The undefined object called *bottom*, denoted by ω, is in *O*.

(c) If x_1 , ... , x_n are in *O* and $x_i \neq \omega$ for i = 1, ... , n then the *sequence* $<x_1$, ... , $x_n>$ is also in *O*.

(d) $<x_1$, ... , $x_n> = \omega$ if $x_i = \omega$ for some i. (Sequence construction is bottom preserving.)

(e) The empty sequence $<>$ is in *O*.

The application of a function f to some object x is denoted by f:x. (The symbol : represents the *infix apply* operator.) All functions in FP are bottom preserving, i.e. $f:\omega = \omega$ for all f. The set of functions in FP consists of *primitive functions* and composite functions.

PRIMITIVE FUNCTIONS

The integers 1, 2, ... (representing selector functions)

k:x produces the k-th element of an object x if x is a sequence of at least k elements. Otherwise it returns ω.

The *tail* function

it removes the first element of a sequence; produces ω when applied to a non-sequence object or to the empty sequence.

id (identity)

id:x = x for all x in *O*.

a, s

a adds 1 while *s* subtracts 1 from its argument.

eq (test for equality)

eq:x = **T** if x is a pair of identical objects; *eq*:x = **F** if x is a pair of non-identical objects; otherwise it produces ω.

eq0 (test for zero)

eq0:0 = **T**.

gt (greater than), *ge* (greater or equal)

For instance, *gt*:<5,2> = **T**, *gt*:<2,5> = **F**, etc.

+,-,×, *mod* (arithmetic operations)

For instance, +:<5,2> = 7, +:<5> = ω, etc.

iota (number sequence generator)

iota:n = <1,2,...,n> if n is an integer.

apndl (append left), *apndr* (append right)

$$apndl: <a, <x_1, \ldots, x_n>> = <a, x_1, \ldots, x_n>$$
$$apndr: <<x_1, \ldots, x_n>, b> = <x_1, \ldots, x_n, b>$$

distl (distribute from the left), *distr* (distribute from the right)

$$distl: <a, <x_1, \ldots, x_n>> = <<a, x_1>, \ldots, <a, x_n>>$$
$$distr: <<x_1, \ldots, x_n>, b> = <<x_1, b>, \ldots, <x_n, b>>$$

It is generally assumed that every primitive function returns ω when applied to a wrong argument.

COMBINING FORMS

Composition: $f \bullet g$

$(f \bullet g):x = f:(g:x)$

Construction: $[f_1, \ldots , f_n]$

$[f_1, \ldots , f_n]:x = <f_1:x, \ldots , f_n:x>$

Conditional: $p \rightarrow f;g$

$(p \rightarrow f;g):x =$ *if* $p:x=\mathbf{T}$ *then* $f:x$ *else if* $p:x=\mathbf{F}$ *then* $g:x$ *else* ω.

Constant: $\bar{x}$

$\bar{x} :y =$ *if* $y \neq \omega$ *then* x *else* ω.

Apply to all: αf

$\alpha f:x = <f:x_1, \ldots ,f:x_n>$, if $x = <x_1, \ldots , x_n>$; ω otherwise.

Insert: $/f$

$(/f):<x_1> = x_1$

$(/f):<x_1 , \ldots , x_n> = f:<x_1 , (/f):<x_2 , \ldots , x_n>>$.

Now, *THE SET OF FUNCTIONS, **F***, will be defined inductively as follows:

(1) Every primitive function is in ***F***.

(2) If $f_1 , \ldots , f_n$ are in ***F*** and C is a combining form which takes n arguments then C applied to $f_1, \ldots, f_n$ is also in ***F***.

(3) If the expression D_f represents a function in the 'extension' of ***F*** by the symbol f, i.e. if D_f is in ***F*** provided that the symbol f is treated as a primitive function, then the function defined (recursively) by the equation $f = D_f$ is also in ***F***.

(4) Nothing else is in ***F***.

Clause (3) has the same purpose as (recursive) function declarations in conventional programming languages. The function symbol f represents the name of a user defined function. The above formalism is somewhat strange because the composition of combining forms with variable arguments is not defined in FP. Combining forms can be applied only to first order functions. Therefore, a variable function name should not be used as an argument to a combining form, nor should it be used as a formal parameter in a combining form. (Note that while functions are always unary in FP, most combining forms have multiple arguments.)

As a matter of fact, the composition of combining forms can be defined as a third order function so we can generate an infinite number of combining forms, but then we have to define precisely the substitution of arguments for formal parameters. If, for instance, f, g, and p are used as formal parameters in the combining form p → f ; g then its naïve substitution for g in f • g gives us f • (p → f ; g) which results in a confusion of possibly different parameters denoted by the same symbol f. A purely combinatorial, i.e. variable free treatment of combining forms is, of course, possible (cf. the discussion of FFP systems in [Back78]) but it may get fairly complicated because of the large number of the individual reduction rules that are necessary for their definitions.

The design of FP was meant to avoid the complications of substitution by using only unary functions and a small set of combining forms to be treated as combinators. The 'extension' of *F* by introducing f as the only variable is relatively simple, since no confusion of variables may occur. This formalism, however, becomes rather involved when dealing with mutual recursion or other more complex combinators.

The most important feature of the FP system is its algebraic nature. This means that FP programs are treated as mathematical objects with a fixed set of 'program forming operations' defined on them. These program forming operations, i.e. *combining forms* satisfy certain algebraic identities that can be inferred from their definitions and from the definitions of the primitive functions. There is, of course, an infinite number of algebraic identities that can be derived in this fashion. The question is whether we can select a few of them from which all the rest follows. In other words, we would like to have a finite set of fundamental identities that can be treated as axioms. The following is a list of axioms proposed by Backus.

AXIOMS

(A1) $h \bullet (p \to f ; g) = p \to h \bullet f ; h \bullet g$

(A2) $(p \to f ; g) \bullet h = p \bullet h \to f \bullet h ; g \bullet h$

(A3) $/f \bullet [g_1, ..., g_n] = f \bullet [g_1, /f \bullet [g_2, ..., g_n]]$

(A4) $/f \bullet [g] = g$

(A5) $[f, g] \bullet h = [f \bullet h, g \bullet h]$

(A6) $1 \cdot [f, g] = f$, in the domain of definition of g

(A7) $2 \cdot [f, g] = g$, in the domain of definition of f

(A8) $p \to (p \to q; r); s = p \to q; s$

(A9) $\alpha f \cdot \textbf{\textit{apndl}} \cdot [g, h] = \textbf{\textit{apndl}} \cdot [f \cdot g, \alpha f \cdot h]$

(A10) $/f \cdot \textbf{\textit{apndl}} \cdot [g, h] = f \cdot [g, /f \cdot h]$

(A11) $\bar{x} \cdot g = \bar{x}$, in the domain of definition of g

Clearly, there are many interesting identities that can be derived from these axioms, but it is not clear whether every valid identity is derivable in this system. In other words, the *completeness* of the axiom system would require a rigorous proof. Also, it is necessary to show that the axiom system is *consistent* and that the axioms are independent of each other.

Note that the notion of a 'valid identity' may be defined in various ways. If an identity is considered valid if and only if it is derivable from a given set of axioms then the question of completeness is meaningless. But, if we consider extensional, i.e. semantical equality as the basis for the validity of an identity of functional expressions then the question of finding the proper set of axioms becomes more interesting. A fully axiomatic treatment of the FP system appears to be rather difficult. It is possible to develop a denotational semantics for FP and use the model for the proof of consistency, etc. This approach has been taken by several authors but the proofs are still fairly complicated.

5.4 Translation of functional programs to λ-calculus

Here we shall define the semantics of FP programs by translating them into our extended λ-notation. The algebraic identities discussed in the previous section should then be inferred from our reduction rules. Indeed, the axioms (A1)–(A11) are all derivable in λ-calculus, which gives us a positive answer to the question of their consistency, but the question of completeness remains open.

A very useful feature of functional languages is their lack of side effects that has been achieved by the elimination of the assignment statement. This makes their translation to λ-calculus relatively simple. As a matter of fact, *many of the well known techniques for implementing functional languages make use of a translation to some variant of the λ-notation and/or combinators.*

The direct representation of lists in our λ-notation makes the translation of functional programs even simpler. Our γ-rules are closely related and have actually been inspired by the properties of the combining form of *construction* as defined by Backus.

There is, however, a major difference between the semantics of the two languages: All functions in FP are strict, while most functions in λ-calculus are considered non-strict. Therefore, we shall use here a non-strict extension of FP.

We can assume that every atomic object of FP has a corresponding atom in Λ. (The undefined object may also be represented by a specific atom, i.e. constant symbol.) Sequences will be represented by lists.

Let us consider first the translation of *primitive functions*. The selector functions and **tail** have obvious counterparts in Λ. The identity function can be translated as the **I** combinator. The test for equality is non-trivial in Λ since the equality of two λ-expressions is undecidable in general. Nevertheless, a strict version of *eq*, which would completely evaluate its arguments to see if they are identical objects, can be designed easily. (Equality is decidable for λ-expressions with normal form.) The function *eq0* corresponds to **zero** while *apndl* corresponds to our & operator.

In order to translate the arithmetic and the relational operators, the ordered pair representation of their operands must be changed to *Currying*. But that is easy. Take, for instance, the **ge** function. The λ-expression

$$\lambda x.((\geq)(1)x)(2)x$$

with our *Curried* $\geq$ operator represents a correct translation of the pair oriented **ge**. Indeed, the application of this expression to an ordered pair [A,B] reduces to $((\geq)A)B$ as required.

The function *iota* can be translated to

$$(\mathbf{Y'})\lambda i.\lambda n.((((=)n)1)[1])((\mathbf{append})(i)(\mathbf{pred})n)[n]$$

which is a recursive definition of the same function in Λ. Similarly, **distl** can be translated to

$$(\mathbf{Y'})\lambda d.\lambda x.\lambda y.(((\mathbf{null})y)[])((\&)[x,(\wedge)y])((d)x)(\sim)y$$

The translations of **apndr** and **distr** are left to the reader as an exercise.

Consider now the translation of the combining forms:

Composition is equivalent to

$$\lambda f.\lambda g.\lambda x.(f)(g)x$$

Construction is exactly the same in either notation. The *Conditional* is equivalent to

$$\lambda p.\lambda f.\lambda g.\lambda x.(((p)x)(f)x)(g)x$$

The *Constant* combinator $\bar{x}$ is equivalent to

$$\lambda z.x$$

Apply to all is equivalent to our **map**, while *Insert* is equivalent to

$$(\mathbf{Y'})\lambda i.\lambda f.\lambda x.(((\mathbf{null})(\sim)x)(\wedge)x)(f)[(\wedge)x,((i)f)(\sim)x]$$

Thus, we can design a relatively simple translation algorithm which produces an equivalent λ-expression to any FP function. The translator itself represents a complete formal semantics for FP, since the meaning of λ-expressions has already been defined by the reduction rules.

The use of the λ-notation as a meta-language for semantic definitions is quite common in theoretical computer science. Its use as a practical tool for implementing programming languages is relatively new, but it is spreading rapidly. This has led to the consideration of nonstrict languages and various forms of lazy evaluation techniques which are closely related to the normal order evaluation strategy of λ-calculus, which will be discussed in Chapter 6.

Imperative programs can also be translated to λ-calculus, but that is in general much more complicated. The major difficulty is caused by the presence of side-effects. It may be interesting to note that *structured programming*, which is a highly disciplined way of writing imperative programs, can substantially decrease the difficulty of the translation from an imperative language to λ-notation. This can be illustrated by the following example.

Consider this program segment written in a Pascal like language:

IF x = 0 THEN x := x + 1 ELSE x := x - 1;

y := x * x / 2;

z := x + y;

PRINT(z);

This can be translated to the λ-expression

(λx.(λy.(λz.(PRINT)z)((+)x)y)((*)x)((/)x)2)(((zero)x)(succ)x)(pred)x

without any difficulty, provided that we add the function PRINT to our set
of primitive functions. Any sequence of assignment statements can be
treated in the same way, because it has a linear flow of control. The IF
statement breaks the linear flow of control though in a relatively simple
(well-structured) manner. Therefore, it can be easily translated to
λ-notation provided that its component parts have already been translated.
Similar is true for the WHILE statement, whose general form is the following:

WHILE (P)X DO X := (F)X;

where P is a predicate, F is a function, and X is the list of all variables occurring in the program. Here the function F represents the overall effect
of a single execution of the body of the WHILE statement. (Some of the
variables may get updated while others are left unchanged.) Now, the
translation of the WHILE construct can be based on its recursive definition, namely

(((while)p)f)x = *if* (p)x *then* (((while)p)f)(f)x *else* x

In pure λ-notation this is written as

while = λp.λf.λx.(((p)x)(((while)p)f)(f)x)x

whose explicit form is

while = (Y')λw.λp.λf.λx.(((p)x)(((w)p)f)(f)x)x

So, the WHILE construct has been defined as a combinator in our
λ-notation, which can be used to translate every WHILE statement pro-

vided that its predicate P and its function F can also be translated to λ-notation.

The translation of an unrestricted GO TO statement is obviously much more difficult. Structured programming is, therefore, very helpful for translating imperative programs to λ-notation. In fact, it represents a first step towards functional programming without abolishing the assignment statement. A limited use of the assignment statement in otherwise purely functional languages has many advantages. The proper discipline of using them may depend on the purpose of their usage.

5.5 List comprehension in Miranda

Miranda is a non-strict functional language based on higher-order recursion equations. It is a trademark of Research Software Limited, and is implemented on a variety of computers. We give here only a brief overview of the language, concentrating on its list oriented features.

List comprehensions were first used by David Turner in KRC, where they were called ZF expressions [Turn82]. They are analoguous to set comprehensions in Zermelo-Frankel set theory. Set comprehension is used in mathematics to define sets via some property. So, for example, the set of odd numbers can be defined as

$$\{ x \mid x \in Z \text{ and } x \bmod 2 = 1 \}$$

where Z represents the set of all integers. It should be noted, however, that this definition is based on the definition of another set, Z, which must be known beforehand in order to find its elements with the given property. The corresponding list comprehension in Miranda will have this form:

$$[x \mid x \leftarrow Z; \ x \bmod 2 = 1]$$

The only difference in the notation is that the curly braces are changed to square brackets, the word 'and' is changed to a semicolon, and the symbol ϵ is changed to $\leftarrow$, which is pronounced 'drawn from'. A more important difference is that the latter is a list, not a set. The same elements may occur several times in a list, but if we want to represent a set by listing its elements in some sequence then we have to make sure that each element occurs exactly once. We are not concerned with sets right now, so we do not worry about possible repetitions.

The list of odd numbers can be defined also in this way:

$$[2 * k + 1 \mid k \leftarrow \mathbf{Z}]$$

This means that the elements of a list may be represented by an expression containing some variable whose value is drawn from another list. The expression may also contain several variables each being drawn from a different list. The general form of a list comprehension is the following:

$$[<expression> \mid <qualifier>; ...; <qualifier>]$$

where each <qualifier> is either a *generator* (such as '$x \leftarrow \mathbf{Z}$') or a *filter* (such as 'x **mod** $2 = 0$'). For example, the list of all factors of a natural number n can given as

$$[d \mid d \leftarrow [1..n \textbf{ div } 2]; n \textbf{ mod } d = 0]$$

which has one generator and one filter. As can be seen from these examples Miranda uses infix notation for the arithmetic operations, and it has a nice shorthand for the list of integers from 1 to some limit like n **div** 2. Let us consider now the most important features of Miranda, which are relevant to our discussion.

Miranda is a purely functional language which has no side-effects or any other imperative features. A program in Miranda is called a *script*, which is a collection of equations defining various functions and data structures. Here is a simple example of a Miranda script taken from [Turn87]:

```
z = sq x / sq y
sq n = n * n
x = a + b
y = a - b
a = 10
b = 5
```

Scripts are used as environments in which to evaluate expressions. So, for example, the expression z will evaluate to 9 in the environment represented by the above script. Function application is denoted simply by juxtaposition, as in sq x. In the definition of the sq function, n is a formal parameter. The scope of a formal parameter is limited to the equation in which it occurs whereas the scope of the other names introduced in a script includes the whole script.

There are three basic data types which are built into the language: *numbers, characters,* and *truth values.* Integer and real types are considered the same. Character type constants are written between qoutation marks, e.g. "John". Type declarations are optional, because the type of an expression can be determined automatically by the system from the types of the constants occurring in it. Type checking is performed during compilation with the aid of a set of type inference rules, which we do not discuss here. But, in order to minimize the amount of type checking at run time, programs will have to be translated to a type-free language. Indeed, the target language of the compilation is a variant of the type-free lambda-calculus.

There are two kinds of built-in data structures in Miranda, called lists and tuples. Lists are written with square brackets and commas. The elements of a list must all be of the same type. The symbol : is used as an infix **cons** operator, while ++ represents the infix **append** operator. So, for example, 0 : [1,2,3] has the value [0,1,2,3], while [1,2,3,4] ++ [5,6,7] has the value [1,2,3,4,5,6,7].

There is a shorthand notation using .. for lists whose elements form an arithmetic series, e.g. [1..100] or [0,5..25]. This notation can also be used for infinite lists, so the list of all natural numbers can be denoted by [0..], and the list of all odd natural numbers by [1,3..]. The prefix # operator is used to compute the length of a list while the infix ! operator is used for subscripting, i.e. selection. So, for example, # [0,2..10] has the value 6, and [0,2..10] ! 1 has 2. Note that the first member of a list L is L ! 0, and the last is L ! (# L − 1).

Tuples are analoguous to records in Pascal. They are written using parentheses instead of square brackets, but they cannot be subscripted. The elements of a tuple can be of mixed type. For example,

("Charles","Brown", 35, **true**)

Accessing the elements of a tuple is done by pattern matching, which is a favorite device of Miranda. It is often used for defining functions with structured arguments. So, for example, the selection functions on 2-tuples can be defined as

   frst (a,b) = a

   scnd (a,b) = b

The application of these functions involves a pattern matching of the structure of the argument with the pattern (a,b). If this pattern matching fails then the function is undefined for the given argument.

It is permitted to define a function by giving several alternative equations, distinguished by different patterns in the formal parameter. We can use pattern matching on natural numbers as well as on lists. Here are some examples:

   fac 0 = 1
   fac (n + 1) = (n + 1) * *fac* n

   sum [] = 0
   sum (a:x) = a + *sum* x

   reverse [] = []
   reverse (a:x) = *reverse* x ++ [a]

   sort [] = []
   sort (a:x) = *sort* [b | b←x; b≤a]++[a]++*sort* [b | b←x; b>a]

There are, of course, many functions which cannot be defined by simple pattern matching. Take, for example, the *gcd* function, which is defined in Miranda via 'guarded equations' as follows:

   gcd a b = *gcd* (a − b), a > b
            = *gcd* (b − a), a < b
            = a,   a = b

According to the semantics of the language, the guards are tested in order, from top to bottom. It is, therefore, recommended to use mutually exclusive tests. The general form of a function definition with guarded equations is this:

f args   = rhs1, test1

        = rhs2, test2

        ...

        = rhsN, testN

One can also introduce local definitions on the right-hand side of a definition, by means of a **where** clause, as shown in this example:

quadr a b c = error "complex roots", delta$<$0
           = [-b/(2*a)], delta=0
           = [-b/(2*a)+radix/(2*a), -b/(2*a)−radix/(2*a)], delta$>$0
           where
           delta = b*b−4*a*c
           radix = sqrt delta

The scope of the **where** clause is all the right-hand sides associated with a given left-hand side.

As we mentioned before, Miranda is a higher-order language. Functions of two or more arguments are considered *Curried* and function application is left-associative. So, the application of a function to two arguments is written simply as f x y, and it will be parsed as the λ-expression ((f)x)y. If a function f has two or more arguments then a partial application of the form f x is treated as a function of the remaining arguments. This makes it possible to define higher-order functions such as *reduce*, which was used in Section 4.3 for a uniform definition of the sum and the product of a sequence. Here we can use pattern matching to define this function as follows:

    reduce a b [] = a
    reduce a b (c:x) = *reduce* (b a c) b x

Hence, we get

    sum = reduce 0 (+)

    prod = reduce 1 (*)

Note that in Miranda an operator can be passed as a parameter, by enclosing it in parentheses.

The alert reader must have noticed the striking similarities between Miranda and the λ-notation. It is, indeed, very easy to translate Miranda programs into our extended λ-notation. A script is just a set of simultaneous equations which can be treated as described in Section 4.4. The right-hand side of every equation will be translated first to a valid λ-expression. Then, in order to minimize the number of forward references, the equations will be rearranged on the basis of the dependency analysis of the given definitions. So, for example, the script which was given at the beginning of this section will be translated as follows:

```
a = 10
b = 5
x = ((+)a)b
y = ((-)a)b
sq = λn.((*)n)n
z = ((/)(sq)x)(sq)y
```

Then the whole script will be combined into a single λ-expression,

$$(\lambda a.(\lambda b.(\lambda x.(\lambda y.(\lambda sq.(\lambda z.E)((/)(sq)x)(sq)y)\lambda n.((*)n)n)((-)a)b)((+)a)b)5)10$$

where E represents the expression to be evaluated in this environment.

The translation of function definitions with guarded equations to *if-then-else* expressions is trivial. A case analysis via pattern matching is not a problem either, as long as we use only simple patterns. Miranda allows more complex patterns, as well, which are somewhat more difficult to handle, but they all can be translated to the λ-notation.

The general form of a **where** close is

```
f  = E₁
   where
   g = E₂
```

$$f = E_1$$
$$\quad \textbf{where}$$
$$\quad g = E_2$$

which can be translated simply as

$$f = (\lambda g.E_1)E_2$$

Let us consider now the translation of lists and tuples. Both will be represented by lists in our type-free λ-notation. Explicitly enumerated lists can be translated directly without any problem. Also, the translation of list comprehensions is relatively simple. Consider first a list comprehension with a single generator. This has the general form:

[E | v ← L]

where E is an expression containing free occurrences of v, while L is a list. It can be translated to

((**map**)λv.E)L

provided that E and L are already in λ-notation. So, for example, the list of odd numbers from 1 to 99 defined in Miranda as

[2*k−1 | k ← [1..50]]

will be translated to

((**map**)λk.((−)((*)2)k)1)(*iota*)50

If we have a list comprehension with two generators like

[E | x ← L; y ← M]

then we write

M′ = ((**map**)λy.E)M

from which we get the result in this form:

(*flat*)((**map**)λx.M′)L

where

(*flat*)x = *if* x = [] *then* []

               else ((**append**)(∧)x)(*flat*)(~)x

This construction can be repeated for any number of generators which takes care of their translation. (Note that an application of the gamma-rules is hidden in this translation, since we map a list, λx.M′, onto L.)

Consider now a list comprehension with a generator and a filter. It has the general form

[E | v ← L; P]

where P is a predicate (true/false expression) containing free occurrences of the variable v. First we can filter out the unwanted elements of L by forming the list

$$L' = ((\textit{filter})\lambda v.P)L$$

where

$$((\textit{filter})\text{test})L = \textit{if } L = [] \textit{ then } []$$

$$\textit{else if } (\text{test})(\wedge)L \textit{ then } ((\&)(\wedge)L)((\textit{filter})\text{test})(\sim)L$$

$$\textit{else } ((\textit{filter})\text{test})(\sim)L$$

Hence, we get the translation

$$((\textbf{map})\lambda v.E)L'$$

as before. For two or more filters the process of filtering out the unwanted elements of the generator is repeated for each filter. On the other hand, if we have two generators with a combined filter, e.g.

$$[E \mid x \leftarrow L; y \leftarrow M; P]$$

where P contains free occurrences of both x and y, then we compute first the list of ordered pairs,

$$V = [[x,y] \mid x \leftarrow L; y \leftarrow M]$$

as

$$(\textit{flat})((\textbf{map})\lambda x.M')L$$

where

$$M' = ((\textit{map})\lambda y.[x,y])M$$

Then we take

$$[((\lambda x.\lambda y.E)(1)v)(2)v \mid v \leftarrow V; ((\lambda x.\lambda y.P)(1)v)(2)v]$$

which has only one generator and one filter. The same technique can be extended to any number of generators, which means that list comprehension can be added also to our extended λ-notation simply as a shorthand (syntactic sugar) without increasing its power. List comprehension is, of course, a very useful tool for the programmer to write transparent and concise programs. For more details on the various features of Miranda we refer to the book [Peyt87].

In conclusion we can say that a translation of Miranda to the type-free λ-calculus is fairly straightforward. This fact may be used for a formal definition of its semantics. Its type system, however, needs special treatment which we do not discuss here. This type system is quite flexible (polymorphic) but still has severe limitations. We feel that the requirement that the elements of a list must all be of the same type is far too restrictive. The calculus we have developed for lists can easily handle lists with elements of mixed type. Moreover, the applicative property of lists expressed by our gamma-rules might be useful in any higher-order language.

Exercises

5.1 Show that the FP axioms listed in Section 5.3 are derivable from the reduction rules of Section 5.1.

5.2 The following is the definition of the Ackermann function in FP:

$$ack = eq0 \bullet 1 \rightarrow a \bullet 2;$$

$$eq0 \bullet 2 \rightarrow ack \bullet [s \bullet 1, \bar{1}];$$

$$ack \bullet [s \bullet 1, ack \bullet [1, s \bullet 2]]$$

Translate this definition into λ-calculus and compare it with its *Curried* version.

5.3 Define an FP function to compute the *n*-th Fibonacci number with the aid of an ordered pair holding two consecutive Fibonacci numbers as an intermediate result. Why is this better than the usual recursive definition? Try to imitate this definition in λ-calculus without using lists.

5.4 Define the function *hanoi* in FP to solve the problem of the *towers of Hanoi*. The function should generate the solution as a sequence of moves denoted by ordered pairs of the form [A, B], which represent moving a disk from tower A to tower B. The initial configuration, where all disks are on the first tower, can be represented by [n, A, B, C], where n is the number of disks, while A, B, and C are the names of the towers. Translate the function *hanoi* to λ-notation. What would you do if you did not have lists in the λ-notation?

5.5 Design a translation scheme for the nested **where** clauses of Miranda, which have the general form

    f = A
      where
      g = B
        where
        h = C
          etc...

What is the difference between the above scheme and the following?

    f = A
      where
      g = B
      h = C
      etc...

5.6 The function *pyth* returns a list of all Pythagorean triangles with sides of total length less than or equal to n. It can be defined in Miranda as follows:

    pyth n = [[a,b,c] | a←[1..n];
                           b←[1..n−a];
                           c←[1..n−a−b];
                           sq a + sq b = sq c]

Observe the fact that a later qualifier may refer to a variable defined in an earlier one, but not vice versa. Translate this definition to λ-notation.

CHAPTER SIX

OUTLINES OF A REDUCTION MACHINE

6.1 Graph representation of λ-expressions

The extended lambda-notation Λ, as defined by its syntax in Section 5.1, may be used as a programming language without any extras. This would be a little cumbersome, because the whole program would have to be written as a single expression. In order to facilitate modular programming we introduce two *program structuring commands*.

The **let** command is used for function definitions, while the **eval** command is used for starting the 'body of the main program'. Actually, these two commands represent only 'syntactic sugar', and they will be translated to pure lambda-notation before execution. For example, a program with the form

    let f = E_1
    let g = E_2
    eval E_3

will be translated to the λ-expression

    $(\lambda f.(\lambda g.E_3)E_2)E_1.$

Note, however, that mutual recursion needs special treatment as discussed in Section 4.4.

Now, for the evaluation of λ-expressions we will design an abstract (hypothetical) machine which would reduce the input expression to normal form. The expression must be stored in the memory of our *Reduction Machine* before the reduction begins. An expression can be represented, in general, either by a *character string* or by a *directed graph*. Thus, we can have *string-reduction* or *graph-reduction* depending on the internal representation we use. Normally, the choice between the two is based on efficiency considerations.

The main advantage of string-reduction is due to the fact that strings can be treated as character arrays, occupying consecutive storage locations, which makes their storage management relatively simple. Certain primitive operations on character strings are also available on regular computers. A major drawback, however, is the large amount of copying that may become necessary during the reduction process.

Graph-reduction, on the other hand, can minimize the amount of copying by using pointers instead. This means that the same copy of a subexpression can be shared among several parts of a larger expression simply by referring to it via its pointer. As a result, logically adjacent parts of an expression will not necessarily occupy adjacent storage locations. So, the benefit of subexpression sharing is counterbalanced by a more complicated storage management system. Indeed, segments of storage used and then released dynamically during the reduction process may become widely scattered all over the storage space. This calls for *garbage collection*, which is a technique for recycling the unused pieces of a fragmented storage. Such techniques are regularly used in LISP interpreters and in many other applications. As a result, many efficient garbage collection techniques have been developed over the years.

The design of our reduction machine is based on graph-reduction, which was originaly developed for the λ-calculus by Wadsworth [Wads71]. It has been adapted to combinator reduction by Turner and others, and it seems to be the best technique for implementing lazy evaluation. The instruction set of our machine will consist of a set of elementary graph-transformations which correspond to the reduction rules defining the semantics of the language. This means that a direct relationship exists between the formal semantics of the language and its 'hardware implementation'. The 'machine code' language of the reduction machine is, in fact, a high-level programming language. The translation of a source program (λ-expression) to its 'machine code' version is nothing but a translation from its string form to its graph-representation. But, that is obviously a one-to-one mapping, which can be easily inverted. Hence, the original source program can be easily retrieved from its 'machine code' translation, which is hardly the case with conventional machines.

The graph-representation of a λ-expression will be built by a simple predictive parser during the input phase. The overal structure of this graph is similar to the parse tree of the input expression. It may contain the following types of nodes:

abstraction (λx)
application (:)
infix list-constructor (,)
list terminator or *empty list* ([])
numeric value (#)
variable (x, y, z, etc...)
combinator (**Y**, **true**, or **false**)
operator (∧, ~, &, +, -, etc...)
indirection (@)
renaming prefix ({z/x})

Renaming nodes do not occur initially in the graph, but they may be introduced during the reduction process. The type of a node determines the number of its children. So, for example, an application node has two children, an abstraction node has one, and a variable or constant node has none. The left-child of an application node is the top node of its operator part while its right-child is the top node of its operand part. So, for example, the graph shown in Figure 6.1 represents the *Curried* addition ((+)A)B.

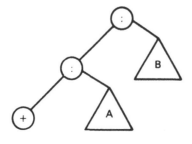

Figure 6.1

The internal representation of a list $[A_1, A_2, \ldots, A_n]$ will have the form as shown in Figure 6.2, where the list terminator node is identical with an empty list.

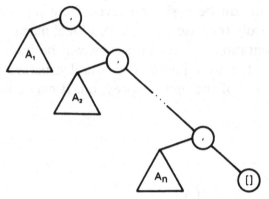

Figure 6.2

So, for example, the λ-expression $((\lambda x.\lambda y.(x)(y)x)2)[E,F]$ will be represented by the graph shown in Figure 6.3.

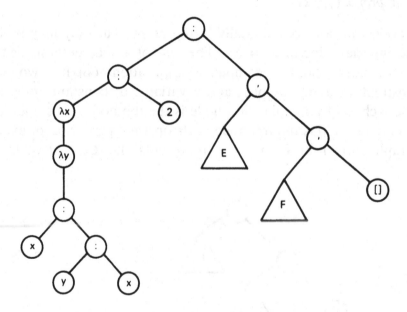

Figure 6.3

The only major difference between our graph-representation and a regular parse tree is due to the *cyclic* representation of recursive definitions. For instance, the following definition of the factorial function:

let *fact* = λn.(((**zero**)n)1)((*)n)(*fact*)(**pred**)n

will be represented by a cyclic graph shown in Figure 6.4. The empty triangle underneath the abstraction node λ.*fact* represents the *scope* of the given definition. The scope may be an arbitrary λ-expression where, due to this arrangement, any free occurrence of *fact* will be replaced by the right-hand side of its definition during the reduction process.

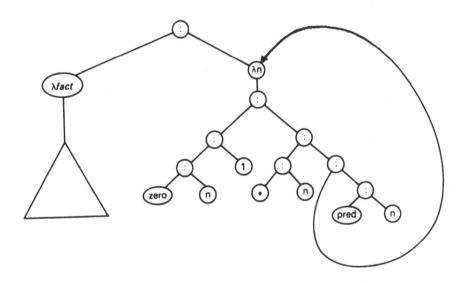

Figure 6.4

Mutual recursion is treated in the same way after being transformed to immediate recursion as described in Section 4.4. This means that the set of simultaneous recursion equations

$$f_1 = e_1$$
$$\vdots$$
$$f_n = e_n$$

(where each e_k may contain free occurrences of every f_i) will be transformed into a single equation

   let $F = [E_1, \dots ,E_n]$

with f_i replaced everywhere by (i)F $(1 \le i \le n)$. This equation will then
be represented by a cyclic graph where each occurrence of F on the right-
hand side of the equation is replaced by an indirection node pointing back
to the top node of the list corresponding to the right-hand side. Recursive
definitions of infinite lists like

   zeros = ((&)0)zeros

are also represented by cyclic graphs obtained in a similar fashion.

   In order to avoid going in circles indefinitely when traversing a cyclic
graph one must take some preventive measures. This holds also for the
output routine which is used for printing λ-expressions from their graphs.
*The output routine which prints a λ-expression in string format by traversing
its graph in depth first order is, in fact, the inverse of the parser.* As a matter
of fact, the same output routine is used for printing the result of a computation which is the normal form of the input expression.

6.2 The instructions of a reduction machine

An elementary step of our reduction machine consists of a single application of a reduction rule. Therefore, we can say that the given reduction
rules are implemented directly by the architecture of the machine. (The
time required for the execution of an elementary step may vary from rule
to rule, but that is not relevant to our discussion.) Every reduction rule
corresponds to some local changes in the expression graph which will be
performed by the machine.

   These local transformations for the α-, β-, and γ-rules are shown in
Figures 6.5, 6.6, and 6.7, respectively. Renaming nodes are created only in
$\beta3$ steps and always use a fresh variable generated by the system. Note
that the γ-rules as well as $\alpha5$ are implemented lazily so that they may be
applied to *partially evaluated infinite lists*.

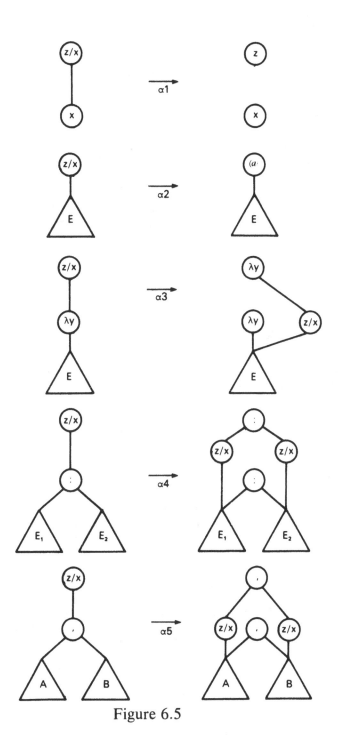

Figure 6.5

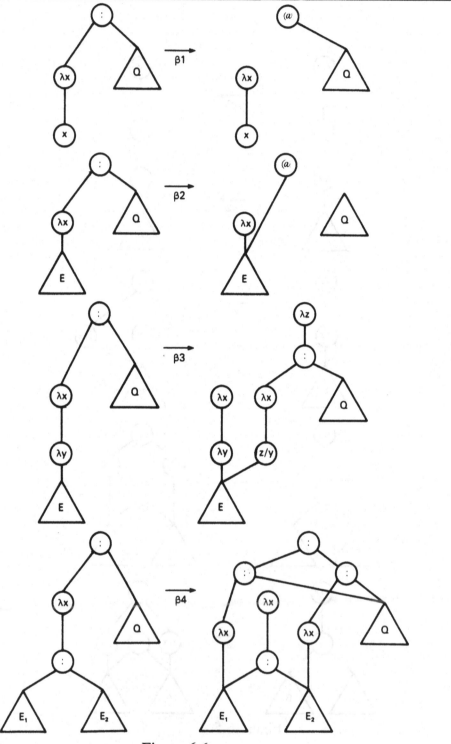

Figure 6.6

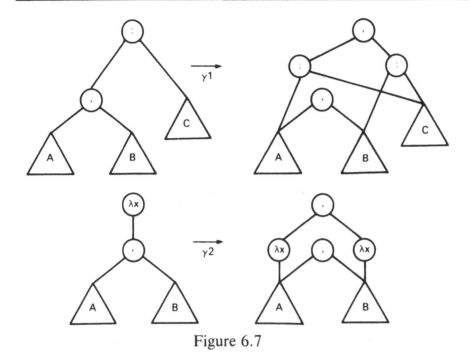

Figure 6.7

It should be emphasized that *the contraction of a redex should not change any of the nodes of a given redex except for its top node which may be changed in its own place.* Therefore, in many cases, we have to insert new nodes into the graph to perform the contraction in question. This is necessary because subexpressions may be shared by various parts of the expression being evaluated. So, for example, if we were to change the abstraction node λy of an α3 redex to a renaming node {z/x} when contracting that redex then this change might affect some other part of the expression which happens to contain a pointer (edge) to this node. But that could change the meaning of the whole expression which is clearly undesirable. In short, the integrity (meaning) of the graph representation can be preserved only if no *side effects* occur.

As can be seen from the graph representation of the β4 rule, the operand part will be shared by the resulting two new applications. But, the *confluent* edges resulting from the application of β4, γ1, or any other rules will never create new cycles. Therefore, if the initial graph contains no cycles then the reduction process will produce only *directed acyclic graphs.*

Note that the initial graph always has a tree form except possibly for some cyclic subgraphs representing recursive definitions. Those cycles can

be avoided by using the **Y** combinator instead. Figure 6.8 shows the
acyclic implementation of the standard **Y** combinator. The implementation
of *controlled reduction* discussed in Section 5.2 is fairly similar.

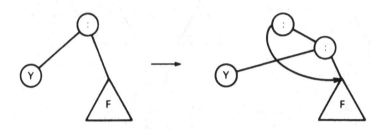

Figure 6.8

Since every recursive definition can be resolved with the aid of the **Y**
combinator, every λ-expression can be represented and evaluated using
only directed acyclic graphs. So, the question is why should we be concerned with cyclic graphs at all? The answer can be summarized in one
word: *efficiency*.

Our implementation gives us the opportunity to represent recursion
by either cyclic or acyclic graphs. We have run various experiments with
both. The size of the acyclic graph tends to grow more rapidly during the
evaluation than that of the corresponding cyclic version. Consequently, the
evaluation process is much faster with the cyclic version than with the
acyclic one. Of course, the difference depends on the given example, but
it is so overwhelming in most cases that there can be no doubt about its
significance. This fact has far-reaching consequences with respect to the
parallel implementation to be discussed in the next chapter.

Now, let us see a bit more closely how graph transformation is done
in our reduction machine. First of all, each node of the graph is stored as
a record with four fields:

| CODE | OP1 | OP2 | MARKER |

The CODE determines the type of the node while OP1 and OP2 are usually pointers (indices) referring to its left-child and right-child, respec-

tively. The MARKER field is only one bit long and it is used exclusively by the garbage collector.

The particular encoding used for various node types is not important as it is quite arbitrary. In our implementation we use, for instance, 1 for the CODE of an abstraction node, whose OP1 contains the name of the bound variable while its OP2 points to its only child. The CODE of an application node is 2, and its OP1 and OP2 are pointers to its children.

The reduction process involves a traversal of the expression graph while looking for a redex. This will be done in a depth-first manner beginning with the root node of the entire graph. In order to locate a β-redex it is necessary to find an application node first. The record of an application node encountered will be stored in a register called N1. Then the record of its left-child will be stored in N2. If that happens to be an abstraction node then its left-child will be stored in N3, and the selection of the appropriate β-rule begins with a search for a free occurrence of the bound variable (OP1 of N2) in the subexpression whose root is in N3. If no such occurrence is found then we have a $\beta2$ redex. Otherwise, the CODE of N3 will decide whether we have a $\beta1$, $\beta3$, or $\beta4$ redex. In each of these cases the graph will be changed accordingly and the search for the next redex continues. However, if the node in N3 is neither a *variable*, nor an *abstraction*, nor an *application* then we have no β-redex here, and we should look for another redex.

For finding an α-redex only two nodes are to be checked. Each time a renaming node is found during the traversal of the graph, it will be stored in N1. Then its right-child will be stored in N2, while N3 remains idle. Similar is true for the two γ-rules.

A nice feature of all these rules is that we can recognize their patterns by looking only at two or three nodes of the entire expression. The rest of the expression will have no influence on the type of the redex in question. The only exception is represented by the $\beta2$ rule whose applicability depends on the fact whether or not the bound variable occurs free inside the operator part of the redex. The search for a free occurrence of a variable in a subexpression is clearly not an elementary operation. It may be treated, however, as a preliminary test, because it does not change the graph at all.

This brief description of the operation of the machine must be sufficient for certain observations. First of all, it is easy to see that the instruction set of the machine is indeed isomorphic with a set of reduction rules. Also, it must be clear that these instructions can be easily simulated on a conventional computer. An unusual feature of these instructions is, perhaps, their synthetic nature, since they are assembled from different nodes, i.e. from different parts of the main storage. Aside from that, the graph can be interpreted as a structured set (as opposed to a sequence) of instructions and thus, it represents indeed a program for computing the result. This program, however, will change significantly during its execution and it eventually develops into its result. This makes reduction machines entirely different from the more conventional *fixed program machines*.

The operation of the reduction machine is controlled by the contents of three registers, N1, N2, and N3. The main purpose of these registers is simply pattern matching with the left-hand sides of the rules. Fortunately, the left-hand sides of our rules have very simple patterns which make them relatively easy to match with the appropriate portion of the graph.

6.3 Implementation of primitive functions

In the previous section we have seen the graph transformation rules associated with the α-, β-, and γ-rules. The implementation of the other reduction rules follow the same approach. Their patterns have been designed in such a way that they can be easily recognized by checking only a few adjacent nodes in the graph.

Each of our primitive functions represents either a unary or a binary operation. The binary ones are always *Curried*, except for the *infix list-constructor*. If we did not restrict ourselves to a maximum of two arguments then the patterns to be recognized by the machine would be more complex. We think that decomposing multi-argument functions to simpler ones is better than using a more complicated pattern matching procedure. For instance, we can implement the S combinator in two steps as follows.

$$((S)A)B \rightarrow (S_1)[A,B]$$

and

$$((S_1)[A,B])C \rightarrow ((A)C)(B)C$$

This way we do not need more registers and the extra time spent on the intermediate transformation will be compensated by the overall simplicity of the pattern matching operation.

Before the application of a primitive function its operand(s) may have to be evaluated or at least examined to some extent. As we have discussed in the previous section, whenever an application node appears in register N1, its left-child will be stored in N2. If that is a unary function then the top node of its operand is obviously the right-child of N1, which will be stored in a separate register called N4.

Consider now, for example, the implementation of the ∧ operator as shown in Figure 6.9. If N4 is an *infix list-constructor* then we can use its OP1 (the pointer to its left-child) for making the necessary changes in the graph; otherwise, the ∧ operation cannot be performed at this point, but it may become executable later if and when the operand gets reduced to an expression which *begins as a list*. All the other unary primitive functions, including the projections, are treated in a similar fashion, which means that their arguments will be analyzed only to the necessary degree.

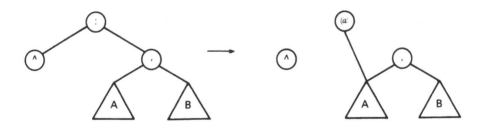

Figure 6.9

The patterns of the binary operations are similar to the *Curried* addition as shown in Figure 6.1. This means that both N1 and N2 must contain application nodes when the binary operator appears in N3. Hence, the right-child of N2 is the top (root) of the first operand while the right-child of N1 is the top of the second operand. If the operator in N3 is either an arithmetic or a relational operator and the operands are numbers then the operation is performed and the result is stored in N1. In other words, the given redex will collapse to a single node holding the numeric value of the result. (The address of the node stored in N1, i.e. the top node of the redex, is kept, of course, in a separate register.) If the operands are not numbers then the execution of the arithmetic operation must be postponed until the operands are reduced to numbers.

The arithmetic and the relational operators cannot be computed lazily (without fully evaluating their arguments), because they are *strict*. So are the boolean operators, as well as the predicates, except for **null**, which is semi-strict. Sometimes, the latter can produce an answer just by looking at the beginning of its operand without evaluating it.

Most of our list manipulating operators are implemented as *semi-strict* functions that can be applied to partially evaluated lists. In order for the function **map** (apply to all) to have the same opportunity it has been implemented lazily as shown in Figure 6.10. This means that the **map** operation will be decomposed into a sequence of its partial applications. The same is true for our implementation of the **append** function.

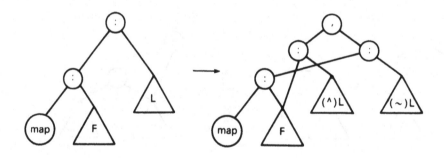

Figure 6.10

The & operator, i.e. the *Curried* list-constructor, represents an interesting special case. It is implemented as a completely *non-strict* function (see Figure 6.11) which does not evaluate its arguments and does not even care about the type of its second operand. Hence, its second operand may or may not be a list. (If it is not, it still may reduce to one later.)

Figure 6.11

The combinators, **true**, **false**, and **Y**, are treated as absolutely *non-strict* operations. They need not evaluate their arguments at all and they can be applied to arbitrary λ-expressions, which makes their implementation quite simple. Observe the fact that we do not make any distinction between the truth values and the corresponding combinators. The same is true for the integers and the selector functions. Fortunately, the Church–Rosser property is preserved under this interpretation, hence, no ambiguity may occur.

The presence of strict as well as non-strict functions has a significant impact on the evaluation strategy used by the Reduction Machine. In a sense, it has to deal with a worst case scenario, because it can never tell when to stop the partial evaluation of the argument and go back to try again to apply the function. The benefit of having only strict functions is obvious. Strict functions can be evaluated in *applicative order* where the argument is always computed before the application of the function. If the computation of an argument does not terminate then the value of the function is considered undefined.

Non-strict functions, on the other hand, may return meaningful results even if some or all of their arguments are undefined. In our situation, we can have arbitrarily nested applications of strict, semi-strict, and non-strict functions. A partial computation of an argument that may satisfy one function may not satisfy another. Moreover, the value of a strict function occurring in the argument of a non-strict one may not be needed at all for the result. Therefore, the strictness of a function by itself does not determine whether or not its arguments should be evaluated. These questions will be discussed in more detail in the next section.

6.4 Demand-driven evaluation

According to the Church—Rosser theorem the redexes occurring in a λ-expression can be contracted in any order as long as the reduction sequence terminates. The problem is that termination in general can be determined only after the fact. Then, how can we possibly find a terminating reduction sequence when some of them are terminating and others are not. Is it just sheer luck when we hit upon one, or is there some better way of finding out whether such a sequence exists at all? The answer to this question is the following.

> **Definition 6.1** (Normal Order Reduction) A sequence of reduction steps is called *normal order reduction* if each of its steps involves the contraction of the leftmost redex of the expression being reduced. (The leftmost redex of an expression is the one whose first symbol precedes the first symbol of any other redex occurring in the expression. Overlapping redexes cannot share the same first symbol.)

Normal order reduction is also called *leftmost* or *outside-in* reduction. The latter term refers to the fact that in normal order reduction every redex is contracted before any of those which are properly contained in it.

> **Theorem 6.1** (Standardization Theorem) If a λ-expression has a normal form, then its *normal order reduction* terminates.

We do not prove this theorem, because it is rather complicated (although not as much as the proof of the Church—Rosser theorem). The interested reader can find a proof in [Bare81]. All we need to know is that *normal order reduction is safe*, as it produces the normal form whenever such exists. So, we do not have to worry about all possible reduction sequences, which is certainly a big relief. Unfortunately, we still cannot tell beforehand whether or not the normal order reduction terminates. What we know for sure is that if it does not terminate then no other reduction sequence can possibly do so.

A word of caution is needed here. The proof of the standardization theorem depends on the properties of the rules used for reduction. By changing any of the rules or adding new rules to the system the validity of the theorem may be destroyed. As a matter of fact, the standardization theorem in its original form is not true in our system. This is due to the fact that our $\beta 3$ rule is more like an intermediate step (a preparation for contraction) rather than a contraction by itself. Consider the following λ-expression

$((\lambda x.\lambda y.E)P)Q$

where E, P, and Q are arbitrary λ-expressions each containing free occurrences of x and y. Contracting the leftmost redex yields

$(\lambda z.(\lambda x.\{z/y\}E)P)Q$

by $\beta 3$. Now, the contraction of the leftmost redex gives us

$((\lambda z.\lambda x.\{z/y\}E)Q)(\lambda z.P)Q$

Hence, we get

$(\lambda v.(\lambda z.\{v/x\}\{z/y\}E)Q)(\lambda z.P)Q$

and again

$((\lambda v.\lambda z.\{v/x\}\{z/y\}E)(\lambda z.P)Q)(\lambda v.Q)(\lambda z.P)Q$

This shows that strictly normal order reduction cannot work here. Actually, it will run indefinitely without making any progress. Fortunately, it is easy to fix this problem. All we have to do is to remember that after each $\beta 3$ reduction the next redex to work with must be its 'trace' that is the one that follows the newly created abstraction prefix λz. This slightly modified version of normal order reduction will avoid the above trap as can be easily verified by the reader. For the sake of simplicity we shall use the term *normal order* to refer to this slightly modified version.

Normal order reduction can also be compared with the so called *demand-driven* (or *call by need*) evaluation strategy which is usually defined by the property that the argument(s) of a function are not computed until their value becomes necessary for the computation of the given function. This means that a 'function call' would not automatically trigger the evaluation of the argument(s). An argument is evaluated during the computation of the function (execution of the body) if and only if its value is actually needed. Take, for instance, the following program:

let iterate $= \lambda f.\lambda x.((\&)x)((\text{iterate})f)(f)x$

let *oddlist* $= ((\text{iterate})(+)2)1$

eval (∧)*oddlist*

This program should produce 1 as a result, which is the first member of *oddlist*. This, however, cannot be computed in applicative order, because the evaluation of *oddlist* never terminates. (It generates the infinite list of odd numbers.) In normal order, however, the redex consisting of the application of the ∧ function to *oddlist* takes precedence over any other redex properly contained in it, which keeps the evaluation of *oddlist* under control. Similarly, the selector function *k* 'demands' only the *k-th* element of *oddlist* and does not need the rest.

Lazy evaluation represents a refinement of the demand-driven approach in the sense that even those arguments which are actually used for the computation of a function will not be fully evaluated when a partial evaluation of their value is already sufficient for the computation at hand. Now, it should be clear that normal order reduction in our system is equivalent to a demand-driven evaluation technique. Moreover, by properly adjusting our reduction rules, we have made it equivalent to lazy evaluation.

The next question is whether normal order reduction is suitable for a practical implementation. Take, for example, the following expression:

$$(\lambda x.((+)x)(\textbf{pred})x)((*)5)(\textbf{succ})3$$

The entire expression is a $\beta 4$ redex and that is, of course, the leftmost redex here. Its contraction gives us

$$((\lambda x.(+)x)((*)5)(\textbf{succ})3)(\lambda x.(\textbf{pred})x)((*)5)(\textbf{succ})3$$

which further reduces to

$$((+)((*)5)(\textbf{succ})3)(\lambda x.(\textbf{pred})x)((*)5)(\textbf{succ})3$$

and then to

$$((+)20)(\lambda x.(\textbf{pred})x)((*)5)(\textbf{succ})3$$

when the normal order is followed. This shows that in normal order reduction the subexpression

$$((*)5)(\textbf{succ})3$$

will be copied in its original form and thus, it seems, it will be evaluated twice. On the other hand, due to the Church–Rosser theorem, it can also be evaluated before the copying occurs so that only its result will be copied. That is why *applicative order evaluation* is considered more efficient. It is similar to the *call by value* technique of passing parameters to subroutines, while normal order reduction is comparable with the *call by name* technique.

Notice, however, that copying in graph representation is usually performed by setting pointers to the same copy. At the same time, the first evaluation of a shared subexpression makes its value available to all of its occurrences. So, it seems that *normal order graph reduction* may represent the combination of the best features of both worlds. It is safe, as far as termination is concerned, and it can avoid some obviously redundant computations.

There have been some studies about the relative efficiencies of various implementation techniques for applicative languages, but there are no clear winners. This should not be surprising at all, if we consider the generality of the problem. We are dealing with the efficiency of the process of evaluating arbitrary partial recursive functions. Standard complexity theory is clearly not applicable to such a broad class of computable functions. The time-complexity of such a universal procedure cannot be bounded by any computable function of the size of the input. Even if we restrict ourselves to a certain subclass of general recursive, i.e. computable functions, say, the class of deterministic polynomial time computable functions, the theoretical tools of complexity theory do not seem to help. Complexity theory is concerned with the inherent difficulty of the problems (or classes of problems) rather than the overall performance of some particular model of a universal computing device.

A precise analytical comparison of different function evaluation techniques is extremely difficult. A more practical approach is to apply some statistical sampling techniques, as is usually done in the performance analysis of hardware systems.

Now, let us go back to the implementation of normal order graph reduction in our reduction machine. As we mentioned earlier, the search for the leftmost redex corresponds to a depth first search in the expression graph. Normal order reduction, however, cannot be done in a strictly left to right manner, because the contraction of the leftmost redex may create a new redex extending more to the left than the current one. A simple example is the following:

((λx.x)λy.(λz.(z)y)f)a

The leftmost redex of this expression is

(λx.x)λy.(λz.(z)y)f

whose contraction yields

λy.(λz.(z)y)f

which contains a $\beta4$ redex. However, the leftmost redex is now the entire expression

(λy.(λz.(z)y)f)a

This means that after each contraction the search for the new leftmost redex must be extended to the left of the one that has just been contracted. But, it need not be started again from the root. It can be done, namely in a reverse scan going backwards from the position of the last contraction. This back-tracking can be implemented by a pushdown stack which keeps track of the pointers to the application nodes that have been left behind while traversing the graph in search for the leftmost redex.

It should be emphasized that we do not have to remember the entire path from the root to the current position, because not every node can be the top node of a redex. Therefore, *only the application nodes will be pushed on the stack* and we do not care about the other nodes occurring in between along the path. After each contraction we pop the stack just once and need not go back any further. Note that this is quite different from the usual *pointer reversal technique*. The latter introduces a side effect on the internal representation of the graph which may cause problems for parallel evaluation techniques.

The only other nodes that may occasionally appear on the stack are the renaming nodes resulting from $\beta3$ reduction steps. They will be processed as soon as they appear unless they have to be distributed over two different parts of a larger expression as specified by $\alpha4$ and $\alpha5$, in which case the new renaming node on the left is processed first while the one on the right is pushed onto the stack. As long as any renaming nodes remain on the stack, only α rules can be applied, which means that every renaming will be finished (no renaming nodes left) before another contraction begins. Again, we have departed here slightly from a purely normal order reduction strategy by assigning the α rules the highest priority. We feel that this makes the evaluation faster, but a strictly normal order is also feasible in this case.

Strict and non-strict functions are treated alike. If an argument does not have the proper form (type) then its evaluation gets started. But, after each reduction step during the evaluation of the argument an attempt is made at the application of the function to the partially evaluated argument. Thus, the argument will be evaluated only to the extent that is absolutely necessary for the application of the given function.

Observe the fact that this behavior of the reduction machine is a direct result of the normal order reduction strategy, and no special tricks like suspensions etc. are needed. This uniformly lazy evaluation strategy may cause a significant loss in the efficiency when computing strict functions. Improvements can be achieved by strictness analysis and some other tricks which we do not discuss here. The whole issue of strictness vs. laziness appears in a different light when the sequential model of computation is replaced by parallel processing.

Exercises

6.1 Design an LL(1) parser for λ-expressions based on their syntax given in Section 5.1. Supplement this parser by *'semantic actions'* to produce the graph-representation of the input expression.

6.2 Design an output routine to print a λ-expression in string format when its graph is given as a directed acyclic graph.

6.3 Design graph-reduction rules for a direct implementation of each of the following combinators (functions):

(a) **append** as defined in Section 4.3

(b) *sum* as defined in Section 4.3

(c) *iterate* as defined in Section 4.5

(d) *curry* as defined in Exercise 4.2

(e) *Insert* as defined in Section 5.3

(f) Y' and Y defined by the reduction rules

$$(Y')E \rightarrow (E)(Y)E \quad \text{for all } E$$

$$(\lambda x.Y)Q \rightarrow Y' \quad \text{for all } x \text{ and } Q$$

Note that the $\beta 2'$-rule must be restricted in this case to

$(\beta 2')$ $(\lambda x.A)Q \rightarrow A$

where A is an atom (i.e. variable or constant) with $A \not\equiv x$.

Implement also the reduction rules for computing with infinite lists in terms of $\mathbf{Y'}$ and $\mathbf{Y}$.

6.4 Design an algorithm for strictness analysis based on the strictness of some of the primitive functions. (How to decide whether or not a user defined function is strict?)

CHAPTER SEVEN

TOWARDS A PARALLEL GRAPH-REDUCTION

7.1 Harnessing the implicit parallelism

Normal order reduction as described in the previous chapter is basically a sequential process. It proceeds by always contracting the leftmost redex of a given expression until no more redex is found. The question arises whether the speed of the reduction process can be increased by contracting more than one redex at the same time. For non-overlapping redexes it seems natural that they can be contracted in parallel rather than one by one without any difficulty. According to the Church–Rosser theorem, the end result does not depend on the order of contractions. So, there is no apparent reason why we should not be able to contract more than one redex simultaneously, provided that these contractions do not interfere with one another.

The Church–Rosser property is one of the most important features of λ-calculus, and it turns out to be instrumental in the design of our parallel evaluation strategy. It clearly implies that the operation of contracting a redex cannot have *side effects* which would somehow influence the outcome of subsequent contractions to obtain a different normal form.

The opportunity for a simultaneous contraction of several redexes depends on the structure of the expression. This kind of parallelism is called *implicit parallelism* as it is determined implicitly by the overall structure of the expression. This is in sharp contrast with the *explicit parallelism* controlled by the programmer via specific language constructs. Explicit parallelism is based on the assumption that the programmer has a conscious control over the events occurring simultaneously during the execution of the program. This explicit control of parallelism may become extremely difficult when the number of concurrent events gets very large. A conscious control of hundreds or even thousands of parallel processes could place a tremendous burden on the programmer's shoulders. On the other hand, it has been suggested by many experts that the implicit parallelism of functional languages may offer a viable alternative to the programmer controlled explicit parallelism used in imperative languages like Concurrent Pascal or ADA.

The graph representation of λ-expressions described in the previous chapter makes their structure more visible, which helps to determine the interdependence of its subexpressions. Also, when searching for a redex, we need to locate only a few of its nodes that are characteristic for the redex in question. These characteristic nodes can be easily distinguished from the rest of the graph and thus, even nested redexes can be contracted simultaneously, provided that they have disjoint sets of characteristic nodes.

The design of our parallel graph reduction strategy is based on a multiprocessor model with the following assumptions:

(1) We assume that we have a *shared memory multiprocessor system* where each processor can read and write in the shared memory.

(2) One of the processors will be designated as the *master* while the others are called *subordinate* processors.

(3) Initially the graph representation of the input expression will be placed in the shared memory. Then the master will start reducing it in normal order.

(4) Whenever the master determines that a subexpression should be reduced in parallel with the normal order then it will place that subexpression in a work pool.

(5) The subordinate processors will send requests to the work pool for subexpressions to be reduced. When a subordinate processor is given a subexpression it will reduce it in normal order.

The most important feature of this model is the existence of a common storage device that can be accessed by each processor. The graph of the entire λ-expression is stored in this shared memory while it is being reduced concurrently by a number of processors. The control of parallelism in this system can be done in many ways. The use of a master processor and several subordinates is not necessarily optimal but this model is relatively simple and it can solve a number of important problems. (This organization has been suggested by Friedman and Wise in [Frie78].)

First of all, the termination of a computation becomes simple in this case. The master can easily determine whether the normal form is reached, because it works in normal order. Moreover, since parallel processing can be initiated only by the master, the amount of parallelism will be limited to a reasonable size. This may sound strange at first, because one might think that one should try to obtain as much parallelism as possible. However, the fact is that there is usually much more implicit parallelism in a large expression than we can handle, and the problem is not how to find it but how to control it. The contraction of a β4-redex, for example, always produces two new redexes which can be processed in parallel. The question is whether the amount of work to be done in parallel is large enough to justify the overhead of initiating a new subtask.

Controlling the parallelism is a very difficult task in general. Normal order reduction makes it possible for the master to delegate work to its subordinate processors in a more or less demand-driven fashion. The selection of subexpressions to be sent to the work pool can be done in two different ways:

(a) Only when it is certain that the evaluation of the subexpression is needed for computing the result. (Conservative Parallelism.)

(b) Whenever it seems possible that the evaluation of the subexpression is useful for computing the result. (Speculative Parallelism.)

Conservative parallelism can be used efficiently in conjunction with *strictness analysis*. If a function is known to be strict in some of its arguments then those arguments can be computed in parallel without running the risk of doing useless work. The operation of addition is, for instance, strict in both of its arguments. Thus, the evaluation of an expression like $((+)P)Q$ can be done in such a way that the two expressions, P and Q, are computed in parallel.

In the case of a nonstrict function, some of the arguments are not always needed for the computation of the function value. But that may depend on the value of the other arguments, which makes it impossible to tell in advance which of the arguments should be evaluated and which should not. (Take, for example, the multiplication as a nonstrict function in both of its arguments meaning that either argument may be undefined when the other evaluates to zero.) Therefore, one can only speculate on the possible need for evaluating those arguments before actually doing it.

The time spent on a speculative computation may turn out to be a wasted effort only after the fact. In order to minimize the time and space wasted on speculative computations, they have to be controlled very carefully. The point is that a strictly demand-driven evaluation strategy is inherently sequential and thus, it is very limited as far as parallel computations are concerned. Speculative computations, on the other hand, are risky, so they must be kept under control in order to avoid excessive waste of time and/or space.

7.2 On-the-fly garbage collection

Graphs representing λ-expressions are stored as linked data structures in the shared memory. They are changed during the reduction process by adding new nodes to the graph and discarding others. Discarded nodes will be considered *garbage*, and the storage management technique for a dynamic recycling of the unused storage space is called *garbage collection*. A garbage collector usually has two phases: (1) the 'marking phase' to identify the active nodes of the graph as opposed to the garbage nodes, (2) the 'collecting phase' to return the space occupied by the garbage nodes to the free space.

In a uniprocessor environment the task of collecting the garbage is usually delayed so that the computation may proceed uninterrupted until the entire free space is consumed. Then the computation is suspended and the garbage collector is executed. Thus, the garbage collector will be executed periodically, but only when it is necessary for the remaining computation. Such a 'stop and go' technique is quite reasonable when we have only one processor at hand.

The same technique can also be used with several processors. This means that each processor would perform graph reduction concurrently with the others until the free space is consumed. At that point they all switch over to garbage collection and then the whole process is repeated. The main advantage of this approach is that the graph will be frozen during the marking phase. The only problem is that the processors must switch simultaneously from the computing stage to the garbage collecting stage and vice versa, and that may involve a great deal of synchronization overhead.

Therefore, in a multiprocessor system it seems better to collect the garbage 'on-the-fly', i.e. concurrently with reducing the graph. Some of the processors can be dedicated to do garbage collection all the time while others are reducing the graph. This approach will largely reduce the overhead of task switching and global synchronization but marking an ever changing graph is a much more difficult task than doing the same with a static graph. (The graph behaves as a moving target for the marking phase.) It is, in fact, impossible to mark precisely the graph when it keeps changing all the time.

Fortunately, as already noted by Dijkstra et al. in [Dijk78], a precise marking is not absolutely necessary for garbage collection. It is enough to guarantee that all the active nodes get marked during the marking phase, but it is not necessary that all garbage nodes be unmarked when the collecting phase begins. In other words, it is sufficient to mark a 'cover' of the graph in order to make sure that no active nodes are collected during the collecting phase. Some of the garbage nodes may remain uncollected in each collecting phase provided that they will be collected at some later stage. To put it differently, every garbage node can have a finite 'latency' period after being discarded and before getting collected.

This last observation was the key to the design of a new *one-level marking algorithm* due to Peter Revesz [RevP85]. His one-level garbage collector works very well for directed acyclic graphs but it cannot collect cyclic garbage. Unfortunately, as we mentioned before, cyclic graphs are more efficient for representing recursive definitions than acyclic ones. Therefore, we have decided to use directed cyclic graphs for representing λ-expressions involving recursion and look for a more sophisticated garbage collection technique for dealing with cyclic garbage. Cyclic garbage is obviously much more difficult to find, because each node occurring in a 'cyclic garbage structure' has at least one parent (nonzero 'reference count').

There are many on-the-fly garbage collection techniques available in the literature that work for cyclic graphs. (See our bibliographical notes.) It seems, however, that cyclic garbage structures do not occur very often in our graph reducer, that is, the typical garbage structure tends to be acyclic in our case. So, we have decided to combine the technique developed for acyclic graphs by Peter Revesz with a more elaborate technique that can handle cyclic garbage. The algorithm developed by Dijkstra et al. [Dijk78] appears to be the most convenient for our purpose.

Consider first the **one-level garbage collector** that works for directed acyclic graphs. This algorithm requires only one scan of the graph memory to find a 'cover' of the active graph.

Assume that *the node space (graph memory) consists of an array of node records which are indexed from 1 to N.* Each node record has a one bit field, called *marker*, that is used exclusively by the garbage collector. At any point in time there are three kinds of nodes in this array: (1) reachable nodes representing the active graph, (2) available nodes in the *free list*, and (3) garbage nodes.

The *free list* is a linked list of node records that is treated as a double ended queue. The 'root' node of the active graph, as well as, the 'head' and the 'last' of the free list must be known to the garbage collector. Initially the marker of each node is set to zero. Marking a node means setting its marker to one. Collecting a garbage node means appending it to the end of the free list as its new 'last' element.

> The **marking phase** of the garbage collector starts by marking the root node of the graph and the head of the free list. Then it scans the node space once from node[1] to node[N], meanwhile marking the children of *every* node.

This means that every node having at least one parent will be marked, regardless of the marking of its parent(s). Thus, all reachable nodes as well as the free nodes will be marked, i.e. included in the cover. Garbage nodes having at least one parent will also be marked. Note, however, that if there is any acyclic garbage then it must have at least one node without a parent.

The *collecting phase* scans the entire node space once, and collects the unmarked nodes while resetting the marker of every node to zero.

As we said before, a totally orphaned node (first level garbage) will be left unmarked during the marking phase. Hence, it will be collected immediately during the following collecting phase. It may, however, have many descendants which are latent garbage at that point. When the collector collects the orphans then their children become orphans (except for those having other parent(s), as well), and this will be repeated until the entire garbage structure is collected. This means that no latent garbage can be lost forever but the length of the latency period depends on the depth of the garbage structure itself.

It is also possible that more than one processor is dedicated to the task of garbage collection in which case the node space will be subdivided into equal intervals each of which is being scanned by one of those processors. The two phases (marking and collecting) of these parallel garbage collectors must be synchronized in this case.

Remember that the garbage collector works in parallel with the graph reducers. This means that nodes may be discarded concurrently with the execution of the marking phase as well as of the collecting phase. If a node becomes an orphan during the marking phase after one of its previous parents has already been scanned, then it obviously remains marked through the end of the marking phase. Its marker will be reset to zero only during the collecting phase that follows, but it will not be collected at that time. During the next marking phase, however, it will obviously remain unmarked, hence, it will be collected afterwards. In other words, all first level garbage that exists at the beginning of a marking phase will be collected during the immediately following collecting phase. This means that all nodes of an acyclic garbage structure will become orphans sooner or later and thus, they all will be collected eventually by this method.

The insertion of new nodes into the graph while the garbage collector is working is another matter. The expression graph and the free list contain all nodes that are reachable either from the root of the expression graph or from the head of the free list. So, *the free list can be treated as part of the active graph.* This means that the free nodes are also considered reachable, hence, removing a node from the free list and attaching it to the expression graph is the same as removing an edge from the graph and inserting another

edge between two reachable nodes. The reduction rules can also be decomposed into such elementary steps that the whole process of graph reduction consists of a series of elementary steps each being either (i)
removing an edge or (ii) inserting a new edge between two reachable
nodes. The question is how these elementary transformations affect the
on-the-fly garbage collector?

First of all, the insertion of a new edge between two reachable nodes
does not change the reachability of any of the nodes. On the other hand,
the removal of an edge may create an orphan. If that node is being discarded at that point, then we have no problem. But, if the same node is also
the target node of a new edge inserted in the process then strange things
can happen. The problem is dealt with in the paper [Dijk78], and it can be
illustrated by the example shown in Figure 7.1.

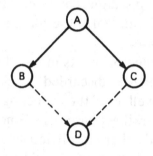

Figure 7.1

Here we assume that the edge from B to D is inserted and the edge from
C to D is removed by the reducer. Assume further that the marking algorithm scans these nodes in alphabetic order. Scanning A results in marking
both B and C. But, if B is scanned *before* the edge from B to D is inserted,
and C is scanned *after* the edge from C to D is removed then D will never
be marked.

Note that the order in which the insertion and the removal of these
edges occur does not matter, because both can happen during the time
between scanning B and scanning C. Node D may thus be missed by the
marking algorithm even if it is has never been disconnected from the graph.
In order to correct this situation we have to place the following demands
on the reducer(s):

(a) New edges can be inserted by the reducer only between already reachable nodes.

(b) The target node of a new edge must be marked by the reducer as part of the uninterruptable (atomic) operation of inserting the edge.

The first requirement prevents any reachable node from being *'temporarily disconnected'*. The second requirement prevents the target node of a new edge from being collected during the first collecting phase that gets to this node after the new edge has been inserted. (The target node must survive until the beginning of the next marking phase in order to be safe.)

These requirements can be easily satisfied by the implementation of the graph-reduction rules. (The order of inserting new edges while removing others must be chosen carefully.)

The only problem with this technique is that it cannot collect cyclic garbage. For that purpose we could use some other technique as an emergency procedure only when necessary. But, a closer analysis of the situation has shown us that the one-level garbage collector can be combined with others in a more efficient manner. The one-level garbage collector places the same demands on the reducer(s) as does the so called DMLSS technique described in [Dijk78]. Therefore, the latter seems to be a natural choice for such a combination. Furthermore, the basic loop of the marking phase in each technique consists of a single scan through the node space. During this scan the children of the nodes are marked. So, the basic loops of the two marking algorithms can be merged killing two birds with one stone [RevP85].

To show how this works, let us summarize the DMLSS technique. Its marking phase makes use of three different markings, say colors, *white, yellow,* and *red.* Initially all nodes are white. The marking phase begins with coloring the root of the graph and the head of the free list yellow. Then the marking phase would try to pass the yellow color of a parent to its children and, at the same time, change the parent's color to red. The purpose of this is to color all reachable nodes red while using yellow only as an intermediate color representing the boundary between the red and the white portions of the graph in the course of propagating the red color to the entire graph. The marking process is finished when the yellow color disappears. At that point all reachable nodes are red.

The converse of the last statement is obviously false, because there may exist red nodes that became garbage during the marking phase after they were colored red. This means that the marking is not precise, but that is not a problem as long as it 'covers' the graph. For a detailed proof of the correctness of the algorithm we refer to the original paper [Dijk78] or to [BenA84].

The reducer(s) must color the target node of a new edge yellow as part of the atomic operation of insertion. (See demand (b) above.) More precisely, it should be colored yellow if it is white and it should retain its color if it is yellow or red. To simplify the description of this operation we use the notion of *shading* a node, which means coloring it yellow if it is white, and leaving its color unchanged if it is yellow or red. So, the basic loop of the marking phase will have this form:

```
counter := 0;
FOR i := 1 TO N DO
IF node[i] is yellow THEN
    BEGIN
    color node[i] red;
    counter := counter + 1;
    shade the children of node[i];
    END
```

This basic loop will be repeated as long as there are any yellow nodes in the graph. When no more yellow nodes are left (counter = 0) then the collecting phase is executed as a single sweep through the node space in which the white nodes are collected and the color of each node is reset to white.

Normally, the marking phase of the DMLSS technique takes several iterations. Nevertheless, its basic loop can be combined with that of the *one-level* marking algorithm by using a three bit marker field for each node, where the one bit marker for the one-level algorithm and the two bit marker for the three colors of the DMLSS algorithm will be stored side by side. Let us use the colors *white* and *blue* for marking with the one-level algorithm. These can be combined with the three colors of the DMLSS algorithm as follows.

```
white  + white = white
white  + blue  = blue
yellow + white = yellow
yellow + blue  = green
red    + white = red
```

red   + blue = purple

Each node can have one of the above six colors. The marking phase of the combined algorithm begins with coloring the 'root' and the 'head' green. The marking of the children of a node in the basic loop will be preceded by choosing the appropriate *shade* for the operation of shading as defined below.

> (a) *Shading a white, yellow, or red node with blue makes it blue, green, or purple, respectively. A blue, green, or purple node retains its color when shaded with blue.*
> (b) *Shading a white, blue, yellow, or green node with green makes it green. Shading a red or purple node with green makes it purple.*

Thus, the basic loop of the marking phase of the **combined algorithm** will have this form:

```
counter := 0;
FOR i := 1 TO N DO
BEGIN
IF node[i] is yellow THEN
    BEGIN
    color node[i] red;
    count := count + 1;
    shade := green;
    END
ELSE IF node[i] is green THEN
    BEGIN
    color node[i] purple;
    count := count + 1;
    shade := green;
    END
ELSE
    shade := blue;
Shade the children of node[i] with shade;
END
```

After each execution of the basic loop the counter is examined to see if the marking phase of the DMLSS algorithm is finished. If not, then the collection phase of the one-level algorithm is performed. (This time only those nodes are collected whose 'blue bit' is zero.) Otherwise, the collecting phase of the DMLSS algorithm is executed, which collects all nodes except the purple ones.

The combination of these two techniques has some interesting properties. Consider the case when a yellow node gets discarded by the reducer and most, or all of its descendants become garbage as a result. The DMLSS algorithm would not notice this fact during its protracted marking phase. Therefore, it will color this node red and keep propagating the color to all of its descendants. The one-level collector, however, will recognize it as first level garbage in the next iteration of the basic loop and then collect it immediately thereafter.

Now, the combined algorithm will color this node red rather then purple during the next iteration of the basic loop. (Its 'blue bit' remains zero because now it is an orphan.) At the same time, its children will be shaded with green. Then the node itself will be collected during the next collecting phase of the one-level collector, leaving its children orphans. But, these children will retain their yellow or red colors after resetting their 'blue bits'. Therefore, the propagation of the color continues through the entire garbage structure one step ahead of the one-level collector. If the garbage structure in question has no cycles then it will be collected by the one-level collector by the time the DMLSS algorithm is finished with its marking phase. The DMLSS algorithm would need another complete marking phase in order to collect this garbage structure. Garbage pick-up is more evenly distributed in time with the one-level collector.

The idea of combining his superficial one-level garbage collector with a slow but thorough one is due to Peter Revesz [RevP85]. For more details on this and other garbage collection techniques we refer to the literature.

To conclude this section we have to emphasize that the free list represents an important interface between the garbage collector and the graph reducer. It is implemented as a shared queue which can be updated by both the reducer(s) and the collector(s). The reducers are the *consumers* the collectors are the *producers* of the free list. The contention among these processes for the shared queue must be handled very carefully in order to achieve maximum efficiency. For more details on shared queue management techniques see [Gott83] or [Hwan84].

7.3 Control of parallelism

As discussed earlier, functional programs present ample opportunity for implicit parallelism. This implicit parallelism is made, in fact, explicit by the graph representation. We will show here that the shared memory multiprocessor system discussed in Section 7.1 represents a reasonable model for parallel graph reduction. So far, we have seen that shared memory multiprocessor systems can be used efficiently for 'on-the-fly' garbage collection. Now, we have to discuss the co-ordination of effort by a number of reducers working concurrently on the same graph.

One of the reducers is called the *master*, the others are called *subordinates*. Each reducer works in normal order using its own control stack. Parallelism can be initiated only by the master by submitting the address of a subexpression to the work pool. The master is responsible also for the termination of a computation when normal form is reached.

The control of parallelism is concerned with speeding up the computation by an efficient use of the available resources. This means that only the time elapsed between starting and finishing a computation by the master is critical. The time spent on the computation by any of the subordinate processors must be within that range and does not matter.

The use of a shared memory makes it necessary for the reducers to protect some of the nodes of the graph from outside interference while they are working on them. An important feature of our graph reduction rules is that the nodes of a redex are accessed in read only mode except for the top node which is updated in place. Therefore, the protection of a redex during its contraction is relatively easy. The processor working on the contraction of the redex must have **exclusive read/write** access to the top node but it can have **simultaneous read only** access to the other nodes with any other processor. This protection mechanism may require a special 'lock' field in each node record, but it also needs hardware support, which we do not discuss here.

In order to develop an efficient strategy for parallel graph reduction we have to address three main questions:

(i) How to represent the *'current state'* of a parallel computation?

(ii) How to select subexpressions for parallel reduction?

(iii) How to avoid useless computations?

The answer to the first question is relatively simple. The control stack of the master represents the main thread of the computation while the work pool represents the pending tasks for possible parallel computations. Each reducer will have a status bit to tell if it is busy or idle. When busy, it will also store the address of the expression that is being reduced by it.

Whenever a subordinate processor starts working on a subexpression, it will insert a special node into the graph in order to alert other processors which bump into this subexpression while traversing the graph in normal order. This scheme was devised by Moti Thadani [Thad85] who also developed the basic version of this control strategy for parallel graph reduction. The extra node is called a 'busy signal' node, which contains information about the processor currently working on the subexpression. Otherwise, this node is treated as an indirection node.

Now, the question is what happens when two processors are trying to reduce the same subexpression. Two cases must be distinguished:

(a) *The master bumps into a subexpression currently being reduced by a subordinate processor.*
(b) *A subordinate processor bumps into a subexpression currently being reduced by another processor.*

In case (a) the master will stop the subordinate processor and take over the reduction of the subexpression as it is. In case (b) the processor already working on the subexpression will continue its work and the other processor will stop, i.e. go back to find some other task from the work pool.

A subordinate processor must be halted also when the master discovers that it performs useless computation. This can happen, for example, when a β2-redex is contracted which throws away the operand. The busy signal node is quite helpful in this case, because it holds the identifier of the processor to be stopped. Note that a subordinate processor cannot initiate other processes, so it has no offspring to worry about when killing it. Of course, the busy signal node must be eliminated from the graph when the corresponding processor stops.

We must observe that subexpressions may be shared and thus, the subexpression discarded in a β2 step may still be needed later on. Nevertheless, it is better to stop evaluating it after the β2 step, because no effort that may have already been spent on it will be wasted. The intermediate result in the form of a partially reduced graph is always reusable. On the other hand, it may involve a very long or perhaps infinite computation which should not be continued until a new demand for it occurs.

Consider now the question of initiating parallel processing, that is, selecting subexpressions to be placed in the work pool. The computation of the value of a function for some argument usually requires the evaluation of the argument. Therefore, it is reasonable to start the evaluation of the argument in parallel with the evaluation of the function when the latter is not simply a primitive function. The master will work on the operator part while a subordinate processor may work on the operand. Another opportunity for parallelism arises when a primitive binary operator such as + is encountered. The master will evaluate the first operand after sending the second operand to the work pool.

A similar situation occurs when a β4-redex is contracted. Again the master will work on the leftmost redex while the other newly formed redex will be sent to the work pool. Similar opportunities occur after the contraction of an α4, α5, γ1, or γ2-redex, which are implemented lazily as shown in Figures 6.5 and 6.7. Also, the lazy implementation of **map** gives rise to an opportunity for parallelism as shown in Figure 6.10. A repeated application of this rule may result in a completely parallel application of the function F to all members of L. The overhead of initiating these processes is relatively small but, of course, we never know how much computation is involved in the reduction of a subexpression sent to the work pool. In other words, this control strategy is based on speculative parallelism which may not be optimal. This leads us to our third question, which is concerned with useless computations.

As we mentioned before, the usefulness of a parallel computation cannot be determined completely in advance when using a nonstrict language. In a strict language like Backus's FP the risk of useless parallelism is much smaller, but it still occurs if, for example, we want to compute the two arms of an if statement in parallel. A serious problem with the strictness requirement is that the value of a function can be undefined in two different ways. Firstly, it may be undefined because the argument has the wrong type or the wrong value as is the case, for instance, with (**null**)2 or with ((/)2)0. Secondly, it may be undefined because its computation does not terminate. In the first case the undefined value can be represented by a special symbol like ω which is, in fact, a well-defined value. In the second case this cannot be done in general, because the non-termination of a computation is undecidable. (A typical cause for non-termination is an ill-defined recursion.)

The strictness requirement appears to be very practical, as it can help to establish the equivalence of the 'call by value' and the 'call by name' mechanisms. Its universal enforcement, however, excludes lazy evaluation and may cause serious inefficiency in certain cases.

Take, for instance, the selector function 1, which selects the first element of a list. If it is treated as a strict function then

$$(1)[E_1, E_2, ..., E_{n-1}, \omega]$$

should be undefined. Now, in order to determine whether any of the elements is undefined we have to evaluate them all before we can return the result. Similar problems occur with the $\wedge$, $\sim$, and & operators. So, the evaluation of strict functions may benefit more from parallelism, because they demand more thorough evaluation to begin with.

The greatest risk of speculative computations with a nonstrict language is due to the existence of possibly useless infinite computations. Normal order lazy evaluation seems to be the only safe way to work with nonstrict languages. Therefore, no matter how cautious we are when initiating speculative computations, they may have to be halted even before the master stops them so that the waste of time and space may be contained. One possible solution is to set a fixed limit to the time and/or space that can be used by any speculative computation.

A very specific infinite computation may occur in our graph reduction technique because of the use of cyclic graphs. As mentioned earlier, each processor has a control stack to keep track of its position while traversing the graph. This means that they do not leave visible marks on the path they travel.

When a large number of processors are traversing concurrently the same (shared) graph then marking off the visited nodes is clearly impractical. (Each node record would have to be extended by as many extra bits as we have parallel processors. Moreover, the termination of a process would require the resetting of the corresponding bits throughout the graph.) The same is true for the 'pointer reversal' technique which is often used in sequential (uniprocessor) implementations. In short, we feel that any kind of side effects (even hidden ones) that store information in the shared graph are undesirable.

The use of control stacks makes it possible to traverse the graph in a 'read only' mode by as many processors as we like. The graph will be traversed via a control stack in depth first order as if it were actually a tree. (The expression graph is nothing but a compact form of the parse tree.) Cyclic graphs, however, may cause some problems. It is, in fact, necessary to prevent the processors from going in circles indefinitely when traversing a cyclic graph. The control stack by itself is not sufficient for that purpose. It will simply overflow without knowing that the processor is running the same track over and over again.

To prevent this from happening we use the following trick. We place a special indirection node in each cycle which must be remembered by each processor when traversed. Each time a processor traverses this node it will ask its local memory whether it has already seen it. If so, then it will back up, otherwise it will keep going but it will remember this node in its local memory. This way it can avoid traversing the cycle twice. This method requires that *every cycle has at least one of these special indirection nodes*. Initially, they will be placed in the graph by the parser, but we have to make sure that this property is preserved throughout the reduction process. (An occurrence of this special node could be eliminated in any reduction step that makes a short cut within a cycle.) Fortunately, a minor adjustment of the reduction rules is sufficient to preserve this property. This has made the traversal of the graph without any side effect possible, which can be done concurrently by any number of processors.

This concludes the discussion of our parallel graph reduction technique for implementing a non-strict functional language. We have concentrated on the hardware independent features and presented the main ideas leaving out many of the technical details. Similar ideas are used in many other techniques developed for the same purpose. Some of the other approaches are mentioned in our bibliographical notes but we cannot offer even a partial survey of this vast area of current research. We hope that future progress in this area will eliminate the need for a sharp distinction between symbolic and numeric computations.

A PROOF OF THE CHURCH–ROSSER THEOREM

The original proof of the Church–Rosser theorem was very long and complicated [Ch-R36]. Many other proofs and generalizations have been published in the last 50 years. The shortest proof, known so far, is due to P. Martin Löf and W. Tait. An exposition of their proof appears as Appendix 1 in [Hind72] and also in [Hind86].

We present below an adaptation of this proof to our definitions of renaming and substitution as given in Section 2.2. These definitions are slightly different from the standard ones. By using these definitions we can ignore the so called α-steps in the proof. In order to make sure that our proof is correct, we have worked out most of the details which are usually left to the reader as an exercise. Therefore, our proof appears to be longer but it is not really so.

The main idea of the proof is to decompose every β-reduction into a sequence of *complete internal developments*, and show that the latter have the diamond property. Then the theorem can be shown by induction on the length of this sequence. The definition of a *complete internal development* is based on the notion of the *residual* of a β-redex.

Definition A.1 (Residual) Let R and S be two occurrences of β-redexes in a λ-expression E such that S is not a proper part of R. Let E change to E' when R is contracted. Then, the **residual** of S with respect to R is defined as follows:

Case 1: R *and* S *do not overlap in* E. Then contracting R leaves S unchanged. This unchanged S in E' is called the residual of S.

Case 2: R *and* S *are the same.* Then contracting R is the same as contracting S. We say S has no residual in E'.

Case 3: R *is a proper part of* S $(R \neq S)$. Then S has the form $(\lambda x.P)Q$, and R is either in P or in Q. Contracting R changes P to P' or Q to Q'. Hence, S changes to $(\lambda x.P')Q$ or $(\lambda x.P)Q'$ and that is the residual of S.

Definition A.2 (Complete Internal Development) Let $R_1, ..., R_n$ $(n \geq 0)$ be a (possibly empty) set of β-redexes occurring in a λ-expression E. Any R_i is called **internal** with respect to the given set iff no other R_j forms a proper part of it. Contracting an internal redex leaves at most n-1 residuals. Contracting R_1, for example, leaves the residuals $R'_2, ..., R'_n$. Contracting any of the latter which is internal with respect to $R'_2, ..., R'_n$ leaves at most n-2 residuals. Repeating this process until no more residuals are left represents a **complete internal development**. The existence of a complete internal development which changes E to E' will be denoted by $E \mapsto E'$. (Note that the symbols $\mapsto$ and $\rightarrow$ are different.)

Any subsequence of a complete internal development forms a complete internal development with respect to the corresponding subset of the given redexes. Also, if $E \mapsto E'$ and $F \mapsto F'$ then $(E)F \mapsto (E')F'$. However, the relation $\mapsto$ is not transitive as can be seen from this example:

$$(\lambda x.(x)y)\lambda z.z \mapsto (\lambda z.z)y \mapsto y$$

but there is no complete internal development from $(\lambda x.(x)y)\lambda z.z$ to y.

The only hard part of the proof is to show that the relation $\mapsto$ has the diamond property (Lemma A.4). This will be shown with the aid of some elementary properties of renaming and substitution which will be established first in three technical lemmas. Then, the theorem will be shown by induction in two steps as illustrated in Figures A.1 and A.2.

Note that according to Definition 2.5, we do not have to worry about α-conversions, because they may occur freely in β-reductions between any two consecutive β-steps and also before the first, as well as after the last β-step. The same is true for complete internal developments.

Lemma A.1 If $S \mapsto S'$ then $\{z/y\}S \mapsto \{z/y\}S'$ for any variables y and z.

Proof. We use induction on the number of occurrences of variables in S, where the occurrence of a bound variable next to its binding λ will also be counted. (This is basically the same as induction on the length of S.)

If S is a single variable then there is nothing to prove.

If S has form $\lambda x.P$ then there is some P' such that $P \mapsto P'$ and $S' \cong \lambda x.P'$. Hence, the assertion follows immediately from the induction hypothesis and Definition 2.2.

If S has form (P)Q then two subcases arise:

Case a: *Every β-redex selected for the given complete internal development is in* P *or* Q. In this case there exist λ-expressions P' and Q' such that $P \mapsto P'$, $Q \mapsto Q'$, and $S' \cong (P')Q'$. But then the induction hypothesis gives us the following complete internal development:

$$\{z/y\}S \equiv \{z/y\}(P)Q \equiv (\{z/y\}P)\{z/y\}Q \mapsto$$

$$(\{z/y\}P')\{z/y\}Q' \cong \{z/y\}(P')Q' \cong \{z/y\}S'.$$

Case b: *The given complete internal development involves contracting the residual of* (P)Q. In this case P must have the form $\lambda x.R$ and the contraction of the residual of (P)Q must be the last step in the given complete internal development. Hence, there are some R' and Q' such that $R \mapsto R'$, $Q \mapsto Q'$, and the given complete internal development has this form:

$$S \equiv (\lambda x.R)Q \mapsto (\lambda x.R')Q' \to [Q'/x]R' \cong S'.$$

Now, for any M, N, z, and y, if $M \to N$ (i.e., M reduces to N in one step) then also $\{z/y\}M \to \{z/y\}N$, which can be shown easily by the reader using induction on the construction of M. This combined with the induction hypothesis gives us the following complete internal development:

$$\{z/y\}S \equiv (\{z/y\}\lambda x.R)\{z/y\}Q \mapsto (\{z/y\}\lambda x.R')\{z/y\}Q' \equiv$$

$$\{z/y\}(\lambda x.R')Q' \to \{z/y\}[Q'/x]R' \cong \{z/y\}S'$$

which completes the proof.

Next, we have to prove some basic properties of the substitution operation. First of all we need the following facts whose proofs are left to the reader:

(1) If $v \notin \phi(N) \cup \phi(Q)$ then $v \notin \phi([N/x]Q)$ for any N and Q.

(2) If $M \cong N$ then $[Q/x]M \cong [Q/x]N$ and $\{z/y\}M \cong \{z/y\}N$ for any M, N, Q, and x, y, z.

Lemma A.2 For any λ-expressions Q, N, S, and variables x, y, z the following statements hold:

(a) $[[N/x]Q/x]S \cong [N/x][Q/x]S$

(b) If $x \not\equiv y$, and $x \notin \phi(S)$ or $y \notin \phi(N)$ then

$$[[N/x]Q/y][N/x]S \cong [N/x][Q/y]S$$

(c) If $x \not\equiv y$, and $x \in \phi(S)$ and $y \in \phi(N)$ then for any z with $x \not\equiv z \not\equiv y$ which is neither free nor bound in $((S)Q)N$

$$[[N/x]Q/z][N/x]\{z/y\}S \cong [N/x][Q/y]S$$

Proof. For each part we shall use again induction on the number of occurrences of variables in S.

Part (a): If S is a single variable then the assertion is trivial. It is also trivial if $S \cong \lambda x.P$ for some P.

If S has form $\lambda v.P$ with $v \not\equiv x$ then we can choose some variable u such that u is neither free nor bound in P and $u \notin \phi(N) \cup \phi(Q)$. Hence, by using the induction hypothesis we get

$$[[N/x]Q/x]\lambda v.P \cong [[N/x]Q/x]\lambda u.\{u/v\}P \cong$$

$$\lambda u.[[N/x]Q/x]\{u/v\}P \cong \lambda u.[N/x][Q/x]\{u/v\}P \cong$$

$$[N/x]\lambda u.[Q/x]\{u/v\}P \cong [N/x][Q/x]\lambda u.\{u/v\}P \cong$$

$$[N/x][Q/x]\lambda v.P$$

which was to be shown.

Finally, if S has form (E)F then the assertion follows easily from the induction hypothesis. Namely,

$$[[N/x]Q/x](E)F \cong ([[N/x]Q/x]E)[[N/x]Q/x]F \cong$$

$$([N/x][Q/x]E)[N/x][Q/x]F \cong$$

$$[N/x]([Q/x]E)[Q/x]F \cong [N/x][Q/x](E)F$$

Part (b): If S is a single variable then the assertion is trivial. It is also trivial if $S \cong \lambda y.P$ for some P.

If S has form $\lambda v.P$ with $v \not\equiv y$ then we can choose some variable u such that u is neither free nor bound in P and $u \notin \phi(N) \cup \phi(Q)$. Hence, by using the induction hypothesis we get

$$[[N/x]Q/y][N/x]\lambda v.P \cong \lambda u.[[N/x]Q/y][N/x]\{u/v\}P \cong$$

$$\lambda u.[N/x][Q/y]\{u/v\}P \cong [N/x][Q/y]\lambda v.P$$

Finally, if S has form (E)F then the assertion follows easily from the induction hypothesis.

Part (c): If S is a single variable then $x \in \phi(S)$ implies $S \cong x$ for which the assertion is trivial.

If S has form $\lambda v.P$ then $v \not\equiv x$ must be the case. Then we can choose some variable u such that u is neither free nor bound in P and $u \notin \phi(N) \cup \phi(Q) \cup \{x,y,z,v\}$. Now, the induction hypothesis gives us

$$[[N/x]Q/z][N/x]\{z/y\}\lambda v.P \cong$$

$$[[N/x]Q/z][N/x]\{z/y\}\lambda u.\{u/v\}P \cong$$

$$\lambda u.[[N/x]Q/z][N/x]\{z/y\}\{u/v\}P \cong$$

$$\lambda u.[N/x][Q/y]\{u/v\}P \cong$$

$$[N/x][Q/y]\lambda u.\{u/v\}P \cong [N/x][Q/y]\lambda v.P$$

Finally, if S has form (E)F then the assertion follows easily from the induction hypothesis, and this completes the proof.

Lemma A.3 If $M \mapsto M'$ and $N \mapsto N'$ then for any variable x $[N/x]M \mapsto [N'/x]M'$.

Proof. We use induction on the construction of M.

If M is a variable then the assertion is trivial.

If M is of the form $\lambda y.S$ then $M' \cong \lambda y.S'$ for some S' with $S \mapsto S'$. Three subcases arise:

Case A: $x \equiv y$. Then the following is a complete internal development:

$$[N/x]\lambda x.S \cong \lambda x.S \mapsto \lambda x.S' \cong M' \cong [N'/x]M'$$

Case B: $x \not\equiv y$, and $x \not\in \phi(S)$ or $y \not\in \phi(N)$. Then the induction hypothesis gives us the following complete internal development:

$$[N/x]\lambda y.S \cong \lambda y.[N/x]S \mapsto \lambda y.[N'/x]S' \cong [N'/x]\lambda y.S'$$

Case C: $x \not\equiv y$, and $x \in \phi(S)$ and $y \in \phi(N)$. Now, for any variable z that is neither free nor bound in $(S)N$, the induction hypothesis and Lemma A.1 give us the following complete internal development:

$$[N/x]\lambda y.S \cong \lambda z.[N/x]\{z/y\}S \mapsto$$

$$\lambda z.[N'/x]\{z/y\}S' \cong [N'/x]\lambda y.S' \cong [N'/x]M'$$

Finally, if M has form (P)Q then two subcases arise:

Case 1: Every β-redex selected for the complete internal development $M \mapsto M'$ is in P or Q. Then $M' \cong (P')Q'$ for some P' and Q' such that $P \mapsto P'$ and $Q \mapsto Q'$. Hence, the induction hypothesis gives us the following complete internal development:

$$[N/x](P)Q \cong ([N/x]P)[N/x]Q \mapsto$$

$$([N'/x]P')[N'/x]Q' \cong [N'/x](P')Q'$$

Case 2: The last step of the complete internal development $M \mapsto M'$ is contracting the residual of (P)Q. Then P has form $\lambda y.S$, and there are λ-expressions S' and Q' such that $S \mapsto S'$, $Q \mapsto Q'$, and $M' \cong [Q'/y]S'$. Now, again three subcases arise:

Subcase 2(a): $x \equiv y$. Then, by part (a) of Lemma A.2, the following is a complete internal development:

$$[N/x](\lambda x.S)Q \cong ([N/x]\lambda x.S)[N/x]Q \cong$$

$$(\lambda x.S)[N/x]Q \mapsto (\lambda x.S')[N'/x]Q' \rightarrow$$

$$[[N'/x]Q'/x]S' \cong [N'/x][Q'/x]S'.$$

Subcase 2(b): $x \not\equiv y$, and $x \not\in \phi(S')$ or $y \not\in \phi(N')$. Then, by part (b) of Lemma A.2, the following is a complete internal development:

$$[N/x](\lambda y.S)Q \cong ([N/x]\lambda y.S)[N/x]Q \mapsto$$

$$([N'/x]\lambda y.S')[N'/x]Q' \cong (\lambda y.[N'/x]S')[N'/x]Q' \rightarrow$$

$[[N'/x]Q'/y][N'/x]S' \cong [N'/x][Q'/y]S' \cong$

$[N'/x]M'$.

Subcase 2(c): $x \not\equiv y$, and $x \in \phi(S')$ and $y \in \phi(N')$. Then, by part (c) of Lemma A.2, the following is a complete internal development:

$[N/x](\lambda y.S)Q \cong ([N/x]\lambda y.S)[N/x]Q \mapsto$

$([N'/x]\lambda y.S')[N'/x]Q' \cong$

$(\lambda z.[N'/x]\{z/y\}S')[N'/x]Q' \to$

$[[N'/x]Q'/z][N'/x]\{z/y\}S' \cong [N'/x][Q'/y]S' \cong$

$[N'/x]M'$,

and this completes the proof.

Lemma A.4 If $E \mapsto U$ and $E \mapsto V$ then there is a λ-expression Z such that $U \mapsto Z$ and $V \mapsto Z$.
Proof. We use induction on the construction of E.

If E is a variable then $U \equiv E \equiv V$ must be the case and thus we can choose $Z \equiv E$.

If E is of the form $\lambda x.P$ then all the β-redexes selected for the given complete internal developments must be in P. This means that $U \cong \lambda x.P'$ and $V \cong \lambda x.P''$ for some P' and P'' with $P \mapsto P'$ and $P \mapsto P''$. Hence, the induction hypothesis gives us some P^+ such that $P' \mapsto P^+$ and $P'' \mapsto P^+$. So, we can choose $Z \cong \lambda x.P^+$.

Finally, if E is of the form (M)N then three subcases arise:
Case 1: Every β-redex selected for the given complete internal developments occurs in M or N. In this case $U \cong (M')N'$ and $V \cong (M'')N''$ for some M', N', M'', and N'' such that $M \mapsto M'$, $N \mapsto N'$, $M \mapsto M''$, and $N \mapsto N''$. By the induction hypothesis we get some M^+ and N^+ such that $M' \mapsto M^+$, $M'' \mapsto M^+$, $N' \mapsto N^+$, and $N'' \mapsto N^+$. Thus, we can choose $Z \cong (M^+)N^+$.
Case 2: E has form $(\lambda x.P)N$, and just one of the given complete internal developments, say, $E \mapsto U$ involves contracting the residual of E. By Definition A.2 this must be the last step in that complete internal development. Therefore, we have some λ-expressions P', P'', N', and N'' such that

$$P \mapsto P', \quad P \mapsto P''$$

$$N \mapsto N', \quad N \mapsto N''$$

and $E \mapsto U$ has form

$$E \mapsto (\lambda x.P')N' \rightarrow [N'/x]P' \cong U$$

while $E \mapsto V$ has form

$$E \mapsto (\lambda x.P'')N'' \cong V.$$

The induction hypothesis gives us P^+ and N^+ such that

$$P' \mapsto P^+, \quad P'' \mapsto P^+$$

$$N' \mapsto N^+, \quad N'' \mapsto N^+$$

Hence, by Lemma A.3 we can choose $Z \cong [N^+/x]P^+$.
Case 3: Both $E \mapsto U$ and $E \mapsto V$ involve contracting the residual
of E. Then the given complete internal developments have form

$$E \mapsto (\lambda x.P')N' \rightarrow [N'/x]P' \cong U$$

$$E \mapsto (\lambda x.P'')N'' \rightarrow [N''/x]P'' \cong V$$

and thus, we can choose $Z \cong [N^+/x]P^+$ just like in Case 2, and this
completes the proof.

Thus, we have shown that the relation $\mapsto$ has the *diamond property*. What
is left to do is to go from *complete internal developments* to arbitrary
β-reductions. This we shall do in two steps:

Step 1: If $E \mapsto U$ and $E \Rightarrow V$ then there is a W such that $U \Rightarrow W$
and $V \mapsto W$.
Proof. Note that every β-step is a complete internal development
in itself. Hence, there exist some $V_1, ..., V_m$ such that

$$E \mapsto V_1 \mapsto ... \mapsto V_m \cong V.$$

Now, a repeated application of Lemma A.4 gives us some
$Z_1, ..., Z_m$ such that

$$U \mapsto Z_1, \text{ and } V_1 \mapsto Z_1$$

and for $1 \leq i < m$

$Z_i \mapsto Z_{i+1}$, and $V_{i+1} \mapsto Z_{i+1}$.

So, we can choose $Z_m \cong W$, which completes the proof.

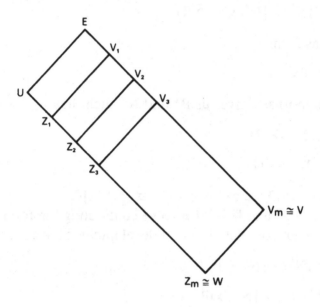

Figure A.1

Step 2: If $E \Rightarrow U$ and $E \Rightarrow V$ then there is a T such that $U \Rightarrow T$ and $V \Rightarrow T$.

Proof. There exist some $U_1, ..., U_n$ such that

$$E \mapsto U_1 \mapsto ... \mapsto U_n \cong U.$$

A repeated application of **Step 1** gives us some $W_1, ..., W_n$ such that

$$U_1 \Rightarrow W_1, \text{ and } V \mapsto W_1$$

and for $1 \leq j < n$

$$U_{j+1} \Rightarrow W_{j+1}, \text{ and } W_j \mapsto W_{j+1}.$$

So, we can choose $W_n \cong T$, which completes the proof.

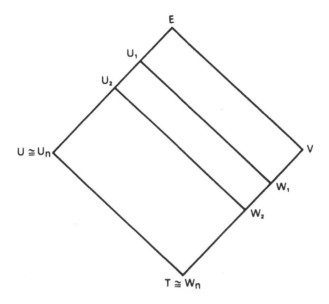

Figure A.2

The result of Step 2 represents the Church–Rosser Theorem for arbitrary β-reductions. It should be noted, however, that the Church–Rosser property may or may not be preserved when new reduction rules are added to the system. If the new rules can be implemented via β-reduction (i.e. they are consequences of the β-rules) then the above proof remains valid. If, however, the new rules are independent of β-conversion then a new proof is needed. This is the case, for example, with the η-rule (see Section 3.4) which cannot be derived from the β-rules. Nevertheless, the above proof can be extended relatively easily to $\beta\eta$-conversion. Such extensions can be found in [Hind86] and [Bare81]. The proof can be extended also to our γ-rules without any difficulty.

INTRODUCTION TO TYPED λ-CALCULUS

In typed λ-calculus every λ-expression must have a type. The assignment of types to λ-expressions is straightforward. First, we assume that we have a fixed set of *ground types* from which all types are built.

> **Definition B.1:** The set of types, **Typ**, is inductively defined as follows:
> (i) The *ground types* are all in **Typ**.
> (ii) If τ and σ are in **Typ** then so is $\tau \to \sigma$

This means that we have only one type constructor, namely the $\to$ symbol for constructing function types. But that is quite sufficient for our purposes, since we have only two expression forming operations, abstraction and application. Next, we assume that every variable has a type. More precisely, we assume that for every type τ there is an infinite sequence of variables of type τ. Then we assign a type to every λ-expression as follows:

> **Definition B.2:** For every τ, the set of λ-expressions of type τ, denoted by Λ_τ, is defined inductively as follows:
> (1) Every variable of type τ is in Λ_τ
> (2) If x is in Λ_τ and E is in Λ_σ then λx.E is in $\Lambda_{\tau \to \sigma}$
> (3) If P is in $\Lambda_{\tau \to \sigma}$ and Q is in Λ_τ then (P)Q is in Λ_σ.

Hence, the set of typed λ-expressions is $\cup \{\Lambda_\tau \mid \tau \in \textbf{Typ}\}$

The notions of free and bound variables, renaming and substitution are defined in the obvious way. Also the β-rule remains the same

(β) $(\lambda x.P)Q \rightarrow [Q/x]P$

except that Q and x must be of the same type. It can be shown by induction on the structure of P that the type of a β-redex $(\lambda x.P)Q$ is the same as that of its contractum. Hence, we can prove that the type of a λ-expression does not change when it is reduced to normal form. This also implies that typing is consistent with β-equality, i.e. equal λ-expressions are of the same type.

It is easy to see that β-reduction has the Church–Rosser property also in typed λ-calculus.

Note, however, that the syntax of typed λ-expressions is more complex than that of the type-free notation because of the extra requirement of type consistency. In particular, if x and Q are not of the same type then the λ-expression $(\lambda x.P)Q$ is not in Λ_τ for any $\tau \in \mathbf{Typ}$. Thus, the set of typed λ-expressions forms a proper subset of the set of type-free ones.

Constants can be introduced naturally to typed λ-calculus by assigning a type to each of them. For instance, the constant 3 is assigned the type **int** and the operator **and** is assigned the type

boolean → (boolean → boolean)

Thus, the operator **and** is applicable only to λ-expressions of type boolean and its application to other λ-expressions is in error.

The type assignment given by Definition B.2 can be used for a preliminary type checking of typed λ-expressions before they are evaluated. This is essentially the same as the static, or compile-time type-checking of a typed programming language. In ALGOL-like languages the type of a variable is usually defined by a type declaration, which is slightly different from our permanent type assignment to the variables. But that is not important, since we can use a different variable in each declaration without any difficulty.

Alternatively, we can make our abstractions more similar to the type declarations of an ALGOL-like language by adding a type specification to each bound variable in the binding prefix. Then the general form of an abstraction will be the following:

λ<variable>:<type>.<λ-expression>

So, for example, the λ-expression

λx:**int**.((*)x)x

will be of type **int→int**, while the similar λ-expression

λx:**real**.((*)x)x

will be of type **real→real**.

Observe the fact that the arithmetic operators are defined on both types, so the type of the above expressions cannot be uniquely determined without an explicit declaration of the type of the bound variable x. This simple example already shows the complications occurring in most type systems. The type assignment described in Definition B.2 is not concerned with the implicit relationship among various types. The 'overloading' of the * operator makes its type ambiguous and thus, we need additional information for a proper type checking.

If not every constant has a unique type then the type of a λ-expression may or may not be uniquely determined by the types of the constants occurring in it. If it is, then we say that the 'implicit' type of the expression is independent of the types of its variables. For example, the type of the expression

((*)3.14)x

is obviously **real** regardless of the type of x, unless it is in error. So, the information supplied by an explicit type assignment to the variables may turn out to be redundant, which makes type checking interesting. It is, in a sense, the confrontation of a 'specification' with the actual program.

Definition B.2 is actually a set of *inference rules* to determine the type of typed λ-expressions. These inference rules can also be used for inferring the type of certain variables occurring in a typed λ-expression. For instance, the type of x in

λx.(**succ**)x

must be **int**, because the function **succ** is of type **int→int**. So, the type of a λ-expression may be well-defined even if no explicit type assignment is given to some of its variables. Unfortunately, it is very difficult to determine in general which of the variables need not be explicitly typed. Many sophisticated type inference systems have been developed for typed programming languages. (See, e.g. [MacQ82], [Mart85], and [Hanc87].)

The type assignment given by Definition B.2 can be easily extended to our list structures. For that purpose we have to modify Definition B.1 by adding the following clause:

(iii) If $\sigma_1, ..., \sigma_n$ are in **Typ** then so is $[\sigma_1, ..., \sigma_n]$

This means that list types are simply the lists of the types of their components. Definition B.2 will then be extended as follows:

(4) If E_i is of type σ_i for $1 \leq i \leq n$ then $[E_1, ..., E_n]$ is of type $[\sigma_1, ..., \sigma_n]$

(5) If P is of type $[\tau \to \sigma_1, ..., \tau \to \sigma_n]$ and Q is of type τ then (P)Q is of type $[\sigma_1, ..., \sigma_n]$

Also, the clauses (2) and (3) of Definition B.2 will be extended to the case when either or both of τ and σ are lists of types. Hence, if x is of type τ then the λ-expression

$$\lambda x.[E_1, ..., E_n]$$

is of type

$$\tau \to [\sigma_1, ..., \sigma_n]$$

while

$$[\lambda x.E_1, ..., \lambda x.E_n]$$

is of type

$$[\tau \to \sigma_1, ..., \tau \to \sigma_n]$$

By applying either of them to some λ-expression of type τ we get a λ-expression of type

$$[\sigma_1, ..., \sigma_n]$$

Here we have introduced infinitely many different list types just as we have infinitely many different function types. This means that our list operators will be 'overloaded' unless we use a different operator for each different list type. We prefer the first approach, therefore, we will use the following inference rules for our overloaded list operators:

$$(\wedge)[\sigma_1, ..., \sigma_n] = \sigma_1$$

$$(\sim)[\sigma_1, ..., \sigma_n] = [\sigma_2, ..., \sigma_n]$$

$$((\&)\tau)[\sigma_1, ..., \sigma_n] = [\tau, \sigma_1, ..., \sigma_n]$$

Similar rules can be given for **map** and **append**, so the type of an application involving these operators can be determined from the types of the operands.

It should be emphasized that *the type of a λ-expression depends on the type of its components*. Therefore, the type of a λ-expression will be computed 'inside-out' rather than in normal order. This means that every subexpression of a well-typed λ-expression must itself be well-typed. To put it differently, 'meaningful' λ-expressions cannot have 'meaningless' subexpressions.

A completely formal calculus on types can be developed along these lines:

SYNTAX OF TYPE-DESCRIPTORS

<type-descriptor>   ::= <ground-type> | <abstraction-type> |

　　　　　　　　　　　　<application-type> | <list-type> |

　　　　　　　　　　　　<operator-type> | <union-type>

<ground-type>   ::=**int** | **real** | **boolean**

<abstraction-type> ::= <type-descriptor> → <type-descriptor>

<application-type> ::= (<type-descriptor>)<type-descriptor>

<list-type>   ::= [] | [<type-descriptor><list-type-tail>

<list-type-tail>   ::=]| , <type-descriptor><list-type-tail>

<opeartor-type>   ::= + | − | * | / | < | ≤ | = | ≥ | > | ≠ | ∧ | ~ | &

<union-type>   ::= <type-descriptor>U<type-descriptor>

This syntax corresponds to an extended version of Definition B.1. The most significant extension is represented by the application-type formed with two arbitrary type-descriptors. The purpose of type checking is now to determine whether or not the types involved in an application actually match. The operator-type is used only for the *overloaded operators*, whose types depend on their context.

Now, to every typed λ-expression we assign a type-descriptor on the basis of the types of its components and its structure.

Definition B.3: The type-descriptor assigned to a λ-expression E, denoted by $(\mathscr{I})E$, is defined inductively as follows:

$(\mathscr{I})0 = $ **int**

$(\mathscr{I})1 = $ **int**, etc...

$(\mathscr{I})$**true** $= $ **boolean**

$(\mathscr{I})$**false** $= $ **boolean**

$(\mathscr{I})$**succ** $= $ **int** → **int**

$(\mathscr{I})$**pred** $= $ **int** → **int**

$(\mathscr{I})$**mod** $= $ **int** → (**int** → **int**)

$(\mathscr{I})$**zero** $= $ **int** → **boolean**

$(\mathscr{I})$**and** $= $ **boolean** → (**boolean** → **boolean**)

$(\mathscr{I})$**or** $= $ **boolean** → (**boolean** → **boolean**)

$(\mathscr{I})$**not** $= $ **boolean** → **boolean**

$(\mathscr{I})$**null** $= \ell \rightarrow$ **boolean**

$(\mathscr{I})$x $= \tau$ if x is a variable of type τ

$(\mathscr{I})\lambda$x.P $= (\mathscr{I})$x → $(\mathscr{I})$P

$(\mathscr{I})$(P)Q $= ((\mathscr{I})$P$)(\mathscr{I})$Q

$(\mathscr{I})[E_1, ..., E_n] = [(\mathscr{I})E_1, ..., (\mathscr{I})E_n]$

$(\mathscr{I})\tau = \tau$ for every type-descriptor τ

The structure of a type-descriptor obtained in this fashion will mirror the structure of the given λ-expression. It may contain, however, the symbol ℓ, which represents a generic list-type in the type-descriptor assigned to the predicate **null**. According to the definition of $\mathscr{I}$, the type of an overloaded operator is itself due to the clause $(\mathscr{I})\tau = \tau$. This clause implies also the assignment $(\mathscr{I})[] = []$.

Type-descriptors can be simplified with the aid of the following rules:

SIMPLIFICATION RULES FOR TYPE-DESCRIPTORS

$(\tau \to \sigma)\tau = \sigma$ for all type-descriptors τ and σ.

$([\tau \to \sigma_1, ..., \tau \to \sigma_n])\tau = [\sigma_1, ..., \sigma_n]$ for all type-descriptors $\tau, \sigma_1, ..., \sigma_n$

$(\ell \to \tau)[] = \tau$ for all type-descriptors τ

$(\ell \to \tau)[\sigma_1, ..., \sigma_n] = \tau$ for all type-descriptors $\tau, \sigma_1, ..., \sigma_n$

$((+)\text{int})\text{int} = \text{int}$

$((+)\text{int})\text{real} = \text{real}$

$((+)\text{real})\text{int} = \text{real}$

$((+)\text{real})\text{real} = \text{real}$ etc...

$((\text{boolean})\tau)\sigma = \tau \bigcup \sigma$

$(\wedge)[] = []$

$(\wedge)[\sigma_1, ..., \sigma_n] = \sigma_1$

$(\wedge)[\sigma_1, ..., \sigma_n] \bigcup [\tau_1, ..., \tau_n] = \sigma_1 \bigcup \tau_1$

$(\sim)[] = []$

$(\sim)[\sigma_1, ..., \sigma_n] = [\sigma_2, ..., \sigma_n]$

$(\sim)\ell = \ell$

$((\&)\tau)[] = [\tau]$

$((\&)\tau)[\sigma_1, ..., \sigma_n] = [\tau, \sigma_1, ..., \sigma_n]$

$(\text{int})[\sigma_1, ..., \sigma_n] = \sigma_1 \bigcup ... \bigcup \sigma_n$

Union-types can be simplified according to the usual properties of the $\bigcup$ operator. Furthermore, any list-type or union of list-types can be simplified (actually 'unified') to ℓ, if necessary. Otherwise, these simplification rules are very similar to the reduction rules of type-free λ-calculus. But, the simplest form of a type-descriptor may not be uniquely determined by these rules, because they may not have the Church-Rosser property. It is, therefore, necessary to prove the consistency of this typing system either by an appropriate generalization of the Church-Rosser theorem or by some other method. (For generalized Church—Rosser theorems see, e.g. [Kn-B70] or [Book83]).

Observe the fact that the application of these simplification rules involves a great deal of pattern matching. For instance, the type expression τ in the simplification rule $(\tau \to \sigma)\tau = \sigma$ may be quite complex. Therefore, the consistency proof for this system is much harder than for standard β-reduction.

Nevertheless, we can design an automatic type checking system based on these rules. After reducing a given type-descriptor to its simplest form we have to check if there is any application-type left in it. An application-type that cannot be simplified must be wrong.

Recursive definitions may cause a problem, however, because we do not have a type-free **Y** combinator in typed λ-calculus. It cannot be represented by any typed λ-expression, because self-application is not allowed in typed λ-calculus. (The type τ is considered different from $\tau \to \tau$ for all $\tau \in$ **Type**.) One possible way around this problem is to introduce a different Y_τ combinator for each $\tau \in$ **Type** with the property

$$(Y_\tau)E \to (E)(Y_\tau)E \quad \text{for all E of the type } \tau,$$

and with the type inference rule

$$(Y_\tau)(\tau \to \tau) = \tau \text{ for all } \tau \in \textbf{Typ}$$

In the absence of fixed-point combinators, *there are no infinite reductions in the typed λ-calculus*, which has the following important consequence:

Theorem B.1: *Every typed λ-expression has a normal form.*

For a detailed proof of this theorem in standard λ-calculus see Appendix two on page 323 in [Hind86]. The idea behind the proof is the observation that the number of arrows in a type-descriptor will never increase during its simplification.

In order to determine the type of a recursively defined function we have to solve the type equation obtained form the given recursive definition. For example, a recursive definition of *fact*, is the following:

$$fact = \lambda n.(((\textbf{zero})n)1)((*)n)(fact)(\textbf{pred})n$$

The corresponding type equation can be obtained from this by Definition B.3. The type expression obtained in this fashion may be simplified by using the above rules. Hence, the type (int → boolean)int

will be simplified as **boolean**. After performing all possible simplifications we obtain the following type equation:

$$\tau = \textbf{int} \rightarrow ((\textbf{boolean})\textbf{int})(\textbf{int} \rightarrow \textbf{int})(\tau)\textbf{int}$$

where τ is the only variable. A possible solution to this equation is

$$\tau = \textbf{int} \rightarrow \textbf{int}$$

which clearly satisfies the equation. The existence of a solution to the type equation does not necessarily imply the existence of a well-defined recursive function satisfying the given definition. If, for example, in the above definition of *fact* we replace the **pred** function by the **succ** function then we get the same type equation, but the function in question is undefined for n > 0. Therefore, type checking is not fool-proof.

Note that the combinators **true** and **false** can also be treated as overloaded operators. Other 'type-free' combinators can be treated in a similar fashion. For instance, the identity combinator **I** may be defined for every typed λ-expression E with the property

(**I**)E = E for every typed λ-expression E,

and with the simplification rule

(**I**)$\tau = \tau$ for all $\tau \in$ **Typ**

The same technique can be used also for the **Y** combinator, which represents, perhaps, the simplest solution to the problem of recursive definitions in typed λ-calculus.

BIBLIOGRAPHICAL NOTES

In order to preserve the continuity of the presentation of the subject matter, references to the literature have been kept at a minimum within the text. The purpose of these notes is to provide additional information on the relevant literature, but the compilation of a comprehensive bibliography on lambda-calculus, combinators, and functional programming is far beyond our goal. Due to the sheer volume of the literature on each of these subjects, we have not been able to include every important paper, nor do we claim that we have listed the most important ones.

These notes serve two purposes, even though they are far from being complete in any way. On one hand, they try to identify the original sources of the material presented in this book. On the other hand, they provide information on further readings for readers interested in some specific area.

There are two excellent books on lambda-calculus, [Bare81] and [Hind86], which contain extensive bibliography and cover a lot more material than our book. But, in order to appreciate those books, the reader must have a strong background in mathematics. They are concerned with the mathematical development of the theory and do not discuss its applications in computer science. A nice introduction to lambda-calculus and its applications in computer science can be found in [Burg75].

A classic on lambda-calculus is [Chur41]. The two volumes of *Combinatory Logic*, [Curr58] and [Curr72], represent the most comprehensive book on combinators and their use in mathematical logic.

The more recent developments in the theory of lambda-calculus and combinators have been inspired mainly by their applications in computer science. Typed lambda-calculus, which is not discussed thoroughly in our book, has been applied successfully to the theory of (typed) programming languages and also made significant progress during the last few years.

The rest of these notes follows the order in which the topics are presented chapter by chapter in our book.

Chapter 1. A systematic study of the fundamental concepts of (imperative) programming languages undertaken by Strachey [Stra67] and Landin [Land65] has shown that the λ-notation is a convenient tool for a precise mathematical description of the meaning of a program. This has led to the development of *Denotational Semantics*, which is the subject of the book [Stoy77]. The tutorial paper [Tenn76] and the book [Gord79] describe the application of the method to practical languages.

The first mathematical model for the type-free lambda-calculus was found by Scott in 1969 [Scott73]. (See also his Turing Award lecture, [Scott77], which tells the whole story.) Another interesting model was constructed later by Plotkin [Plot76].

Polymorphic functions have become quite popular in type theory lately due to the investigations started by Girard [Gira71] and Reynolds [Reyn74]. A good introduction to the type theory of progamming languages is [Ca-W85]. For more information on type theory see also Chapters 15 and 16 in [Hind86].

Chapter 2. Our definitions of *renaming* and *substitution* are slightly modified versions of the standard definitions. The Church–Rosser theorem was published first in [Ch-R36]. The revised α-, and β-rules discussed in Section 2.5 are from [RevG85]. There are many alternative definitions of β-reduction, most of which have been designed for being implementated on a computer rather than being used by people. The best known are [DeBr72], [Berk82], and [Stap79].

Chapter 3. The standard combinators were discovered independently by Schönfinkel [Schö24] and Curry [Curr30]. The **Y** combinator was called the *paradoxical combinator* by Curry, because it leads to a paradox when used in mathematical logic. This has prevented both the λ-calculus and the theory combinators from being used as a foundation for mathematics, which was the original goal of their development [Ross82]. The close relationship between λ-calculus and the theory of recursive functions is well explained in [Klee81].

The most significant improvements on the algorithm for bracket abstraction, i.e. translation from the λ-notation to pure combinators, have been achieved so far by Abdali [Abda76] and Turner [Turn79a]. Turner's combinators have been used for implementing functional languages as described in [Turn79b] and [Sche86]. As can be seen from [Burt82] and [Nosh85], bracket abstraction still represents one of the most difficult problems for an efficienct use of combinators. Hughes suggested using program dependent combinators, which he called super-combinators, rather than a fixed set of predefined combinators [Hugh82]. Hudak and Goldberg further refined the notion of super-combinators in [Huda85]. A hardware design based on standard combinators is presented in [Clar80]. The design of the G-machine is based on the super-combinator approach [Kieb85]. An interesting hardware design for implementing combinators is described in [Rams86].

Chapter 4. The extension of the λ-notation to include lists as primitive objects was given in [RevG84]. The $\alpha5$-rule, as well as the γ-rules are from the same paper. The latter are clearly independent of the β-rules and they are not valid for the 'encoded' representation of lists described at the beginning of Chapter 4. Our treatment of mutual recursion is from [RevG87].

The use of lazy evaluation for dealing with infinite lists has been suggested by many authors. We have been influenced mainly by [Turn82]. Sequential input or output files can also be treated as infinite lists. If applicative order is used as the standard evaluation technique then they need special treatment. In this case, they are usually considered as special objects, called *streams*, which must be processed with *delayed evaluation,* or *suspension,* etc. (See, for example, Section 3.4 in [Abel85].)

Chapter 5. One of the major advantages of functional languages is that their semantics can be described in terms of rewriting rules [Halp84]. The same is true, of course, for the lambda-calculus, which represents, in fact, a model of computation equivalent to the Turing machine. It should be noted, however, that many authors treat β-conversion as a purely syntactic matter. They consider the construction of an independent mathematical model based on set theory (or some other algebraic structure) as the only proper way of defining the semantics of lambda-calculus. There is some truth in this view, but it has never been applied to Turing machines whose meaning was thought to be intuitively clear. This author feels that lambda-calculus as a purely formal system for performing reductions, i.e. mechanical computations, is self-sufficient. A naïve interpretation of λ-expressions is, of course, another matter. It was indeed necessary to clarify what kinds of interpretations are reasonable and what are not [Scott73]. At the same time, the discovery of Scott-continuous functions has made it possible to find a purely extensional characterization of computable functions, which is explained in more details in [Stoy77].

Controlled reduction is introduced in [RevG87]. It is related to the idea of suspension or delayed execution used by many authors following a suggestion by Friedman and Wise [Frie76]. The difference between our controlled reduction and those other approaches is that we achieve the effect of suspension by an appropriate modification of the reduction rules themselves rather than by some extraneous control mechanism.

The FP system was designed by Backus [Back78], who has had the most significant impact on the development of functional style programming. A formal semantics for functional programs has been developed by Williams [Will82]. A translator from FP to our extended λ-notation has been implemented by Cazes [Caze87].

A thorough discussion of the design and implementation of Miranda can be found in the book [Peyt87]. Our description of Miranda is based on [Turn87], which appears as the Appendix in the same book.

Chapter 6. Graph reduction techniques have been studied by several authors. The effect of sharing is analyzed in [Arvi85], which contains references to many other papers on graph reduction. Our graph reduction rules discussed in this chapter are from [RevG84]. A cyclic representation of recursion equations has been suggested by Turner [Turn79b]. Many other graph reduction techniques have been developed for implementing functional languages. (See, for example, [Thak86].) Most of them are using combinators rather than lambda-expressions. One of the most promising efforts was the development of NORMA (Normal Order

Reduction Machine) [Sche86], but it has been dropped. Graph reduction is discussed at length in [Peyt87].

The survey paper [Vegd84] is a fairly complete account of various implementation techniques that have been developed for functional languages. The so called *data flow* approach is somewhat complementary to graph reduction [Ager82], because it proceeds from bottom up rather than top down in the expression graph. But, it does not change the graph, so it is a *fixed program approach* while graph reduction is not. An interesting technique for parallel string reduction has been developed by Mago [Mago79].

Chapter 7. A preliminary version of our parallel graph reduction strategy is described in [Thad85]. More about on-the-fly garbage collection can be found in [Cohe81]. The parallel graph reduction technique described in [Clac86] is somewhat similar to ours, but it has some very important differences. More about implementing functional languages can be found in [Hend80] and [Peyt87].

REFERENCES

[Abda76] ABDALI, S. K. An abstraction algorithm for combinatory logic, *The Journal of Symbolic Logic* Vol.41, No.1, (March 1976), pp. 222-224.

[Abel85] ABELSON, H., and SUSSMAN, G. J. with SUSSMAN, J., *Structure and Interpretation of Computer Programs*, MIT Press, and McGraw-Hill Book Company, 1985.

[Ager82] AGERWALA, T., and ARVIND: Data Flow Systems, *Computer* 15, 2 (1982), pp. 10-13.

[Arvi85] ARVIND, KATHAIL, V., and PINGALI K., Sharing computation in functional language implementations, *Proc. Internat. Workshop on High-level Computer Architecture,* Los Angeles, May 21-25, 1985, pp. 5.1-5.12.

[Back78] BACKUS, J. W., Can programming be liberated from the von Neumann style? A functional style and its algebra of programs. *Communications of the ACM,* Vol. 21, No. 8, (August 1978), pp. 613-641.

[Bare81] BARENDREGT, H. P., *The Lambda Calculus: Its Syntax and Semantics.* 1st ed., North-Holland, 1981, 2nd ed., North-Holland, 1984.

[BenA84] BEN-ARI, M., Algorithms for on-the-fly garbage collection. *ACM Trans. Prog. Lang. Sys.*, Vol. 6, No. 3, (July 1984), pp. 333-345.

[Berk82] BERKLING, K. J., and FEHR, E., A modification of the λ-calculus as a base for functional programming languages. *Proc. 9th ICALP Conference*, Lecture Notes in Computer Science, Vol. 140, Springer-Verlag, (1982), pp. 35-47.

[Book83] BOOK, R. V., Thue systems and the Church–Rosser property. *Combinatorics on Words: Progress and Perspectives*, (ed. Cummings, L. J.) Academic Press, pp. 1-38.

[Burg75] BURGE, W., *Recursive Programming Techniques*, Addison-Wesley, 1975.

[Burt82] BURTON, F. W, A linear space translation of functional programs to Turner combinators, *Information Processing Letters*, Vol.14, No.5, 1982, pp. 201-204.

[Ca-W85] CARDELLI, L., and WEGNER, P., On understanding types, data abstraction, and polymorphism. *Computing Surveys* Vol. 17, No. 4, (December 1985), pp. 471-522.

[Caze87] CAZES, A., A translator from FP to the lambda calculus. *Research Report*, No. RC 12844, IBM Thomas J. Watson Research Center, Yorktown Heights, New York, 1987.

[Chur41] CHURCH, A. *The Calculi of Lambda Conversion* Princeton University Press, Princeton, N.J., 1941.

[Ch-R36] CHURCH, A., and ROSSER, J. B., Some properties of conversion. *Trans. Amer. Math. Soc.*, Vol. 39. (1936), pp. 472-482.

[Clac86] CLACK, C., and PEYTON-JONES, S. L., The four stroke reduction engine. *Proc. of the 1986 ACM Conference on LISP and Functional Programming*, Cambridge, Mass. (Aug. 1986), pp. 220-232.

[Clar80] CLARKE, T. J. W, GLADSTONE, P. J. S., MACLEAN, C. D., and NORMAN, A. C., SKIM - The S, K, I, reduction machine. *LISP Conference Records*, Stanford University, Stanford, CA 1980, pp. 128-135.

[Cohe81] COHEN, J., Garbage collection of linked data structures. *Computing Surveys*, Vol. 13, No. 3, (Sept. 1981), pp. 341-367.

[Curr30] CURRY, H. B., Grundlagen der kombinatorischen Logik. *American J. Math.*, Vol. 52, (1930), pp. 509-536, 789-834.

[Curr58] CURRY, H. B., and FEYS, R., *Combinatory Logic, Vol. I,* North-Holland, Amsterdam, 1958.

[Curr72] CURRY, H. B., HINDLEY, J. R., and SELDIN, J. P., *Combinatory Logic, Vol. II,* North-Holland, Amsterdam, 1972.

[DeBr72] De BRUIJN, N. G., Lambda-calculus notation with nameles dummies, a tool for automatic formula manipulation with application to the Church-Rosser theorem. *Indag. Math.*, Vol. 34, (1972), pp. 381-392.

[Dijk78] DIJKSTRA, E. W., LAMPORT. L., MARTIN, A. J., SCHOLTEN, C. S., and STEFFENS, E. F. M., On-the-fly garbage collection: An exercise in cooperation. *Communications of the ACM, vol. 21, no. 11,* November 1978, pp. 966-975.

[Frie76] FRIEDMAN, D. P., and WISE, D. S., Cons should not evaluate its arguments. *Automata, Languages, and Programming,* (ed. MICHELSON, S., and MILNER, J.), Edinburgh Univ. Press, Edinburgh (1976), pp. 257-284.

[Frie78] FRIEDMAN, D. P., and WISE, D. S., Aspects of applicative programming for parallel processing. *IEEE Trans. Comput.,* **C-27**, (April 1978), pp. 289-296.

[Gira71] GIRARD, J-Y., Une extension de l'interprétation de Gödel à l'analyse et son application à l'élimination des coupures dans l'analyse et la théorie des types. *Proceedings of the Second Scandinavian Logic Symposium,* (ed. FENSTAD, J. E.), North-Holland, 1971, pp. 63-92.

[Gott83] GOTTLIEB, A., LUBACHEVSKY, B. D., and RUDOLPH, L., Coordination of very large number of processors. *ACM Transactions on Programming Languages and Systems, 5(2),* April 1983, pp. 164-189.

[Gord79] GORDON, M. J. C., *The Denotational Description of Programming Languages,* Springer-Verlag, 1979.

[Halp84] HALPERN, J. Y., WILLIAMS, J. H., WIMMERS, E. L., and WINKLER, T. C., Denotational semantics and rewrite rules for FP. *Conf. Rec. 12th Annual ACM Symposium on Principles of Programming Languages,* New Orleans, LA (1985), pp. 108-120.

[Hanc87] HANCOCK, P., Polymorphic type-checking. *Chapter 9 in* [Peyt87], pp. 139-182.

[Hend80] HENDERSON, P., *Functional Programming: Application and Implementation,* Prentice-Hall, 1980.

[Hind72] HINDLEY, J. R., LERCHER, B., and SELDIN, J. P., *Introduction to Combinatory Logic,* Cambridge University Press, London, 1972.

[Hind86] HINDLEY, J. R., and SELDIN, J. P., *Introduction to Combinators and λ-Calculus.* Cambridge University Press, 1986.

[Huda85] HUDAK, P., and GOLDBERG, B., Distributed execution of functional programs using serial combinators. *IEEE Transaction on Computers,* **C-34**(10), (October 1985), pp. 881-891.

[Hugh82] HUGHES, R. J. M., Super-combinators: A new implementation method for applicative languages. *Conf. Rec. 1982 ACM Symposium on LISP and Functional Programming*, Carnegie-Mellon Univ., Pittsburgh, PA, (Aug. 1982), pp. 1-10.

[Hwan84] HWANG, K., and BRIGGS, R., *Computer Architecture and Parallel Processing*. McGraw-Hill, 1984.

[Kieb85] KIEBURTZ, R. B., The G-machine: a fast, graph-reduction evaluator. *Proc. of IFIP Conf. on Functional Prog. Lang. and Computer Arch.*, Nancy, 1985, pp. 400-413.

[Klee81] KLEENE, S. C., Origins of recursive function theory. *Annals of the History of Computing*, Vol. 3, No. 1, (January 1981), pp. 52-67.

[Kn-B70] KNUTH, D. E. and BENDIX, P., Simple word problems in universal algebras. *Computational Problems in Abstract Algebra*, (ed. Leech, J.) Pergamon Press, Oxford (1970), pp. 263-297.

[Land65] LANDIN, P. J., A correspondance between Algol 60 and Church's lambda-notation. *Communications of the ACM*, Vol. 8, (1965), pp. 89-101, 158-165.

[MacQ82] MACQUEEN, D. and SETHI, R., A semantic model of types for applicative languages. *Conference Record of the 1982 ACM Symposium on Lisp and Functional Programming*, pp. 243-252.

[Mago79] MAGO, G. A., A network of microprocessors to execute reduction languages, Part 1 and Part 2. *International Journal of Computer and Information Sciences*, Vol.8, No.5, (1979) pp. 349-385, and Vol.8, No.6, (1979) pp. 435-471.

[Mart85] MARTIN-LÖF, P., Constructive mathematics and computer programming. *Mathematical Logic and Programming Languages*, (ed. Hoare, C. A. R. and Shepherdson, J. C.), Prentice-Hall, 1985, pp.167-184.

[Nosh85] NOSHITA, K, and HIKITA, T., The BC-chain method for representing combinators in linear space. *New Generation Computing*, Vol.3, 1985, pp. 131-144.

[Peyt87] PEYTON-JONES, S. L., *The Implementation of Functional Languages*, Prentice-Hall, 1987.

[Plot76] PLOTKIN, G. D., A powerdomain construction. *SIAM Journal on Computing*, Vol. 5, (1976), pp. 452-487.

[Rams86] RAMSDELL, J. D., The CURRY Chip. *Proc. of the 1986 ACM Conference on LISP and Functional Programming*, Cambridge, Mass. (Aug.1986), pp. 122-131.

[RevG84] REVESZ, G., An extension of lambda-calculus for functional programming, *The Journal of Logic Programming,* Vol.1, No.3, (1984), pp. 241-251.

[RevG85] REVESZ, G., Axioms for the theory of lambda-conversion, *SIAM Journal on Computing,* Vol.14, No.2, (1985), pp. 373-382.

[RevG87] REVESZ, G., Rule-based semantics for an extended λ-calculus. *Research Report,* No. RC 12570, IBM Thomas J. Watson Research Center, Yorktown Heights, New York, 1987.

[RevP85] REVESZ, P. Z., A new parallel garbage collection algorithm. *Honor's Thesis,* Tulane University, New Orleans, 1985.

[Reyn74] REYNOLDS, J. C., Towards a theory of type structure. *Lecture Notes in Computer Science,* Vol. 19, Springer-Verlag, 1974, pp. 408-425.

[Ross82] ROSSER, J. B., Highlights of the history of the lambda-calculus. *Conference Record of the 1982 ACM Conference on LISP and Functional Programming,* Pittsburgh, Pennsylvania, (Aug. 1982), pp. 216-225.

[Sche86] SCHEEVEL, M., NORMA: A graph reduction processor. *Proc. of the 1986 ACM Conference on LISP and Functional Programming,* Cambridge, Mass. (Aug. 1986), pp. 212-219.

[Schö24] SCHÖNFINKEL, M., Über die Bausteine der mathematischen Logik. *Math. Annalen,* Vol. 92, (1924), pp. 305-316.

[Scott73] SCOTT, D. S., Models for Various Type-free Calculi. *Logic, Methodology and Philosophy of Science IV,* (ed. SUPPES et al.), North-Holland, 1973, pp.157-187.

[Scott77] SCOTT, D. S., Logic and programming languages. *Communications of the ACM,* Vol. 20, No. 9, (September 1977), pp. 634-641.

[Scott80] SCOTT, D. S., Relating theories of the λ-calculus. *To H. B. Curry: Essays on Combinatory Logic, Lambda Calculus and Formalism,* (ed. SELDIN, J. P. and HINDLEY, J. R.), Academic Press, 1980.

[Stap79] STAPLES, J., A lambda calculus with naïve substitution, *J. Austral. Math. Soc.* Ser. A, 28 (1979), pp. 269-282.

[Stoy77] STOY, J. E., *Denotational Semantics: The Scott-Strachey Approach to Programming Language Theory,* MIT press, 1977.

[Stra67] STRACHEY, C., Fundamental concepts in programming languages. *International Summer School in Computer Programming,* Copenhagen, 1967, (unpublished)

[Tenn76] TENNENT, R. D., The denotational semantics of programming languages. *Communications of the ACM*, Vol. 19, No. 8, (1976), pp.437-453.

[Thad85] THADANI, M., Parallelism in reduction machines. *Master's Thesis*, Tulane University, New Orleans, LA, 1985.

[Thak86] THAKKAR, S. S., and HOSTMANN, W. E., An instruction fetch unit for a graph reduction machine. *IEEE Computer Architecture Conference 1986*, pp. 82-90.

[Turn79a] TURNER, D. A., Another algorithm for bracket abstraction. *Journal of Symbolic Logic*, Vol.44, No.2, (June 1979), pp. 267-270.

[Turn79b] TURNER, D. A., A new implementation technique for applicative languages. *Software - Practice and Experience*, Vol.9, (Sept. 1979), pp. 31-49.

[Turn82] TURNER, D. A., Recursion equations as a programming language. *Functional Programming and its Applications*, (ed. DARLINGTON et al.), Cambridge University Press, 1982, pp. 1-28.

[Turn87] TURNER, D. A., An introduction to Miranda. *Appendix* to [Peyt87], pp. 431-438.

[Vegd84] VEGDAHL, S. R., A survey of proposed architectures for the execution of functional languages. *IEEE Transactions on Computers*, C-33(12), (December 1984), pp. 1050-1071.

[Wads71] WADSWORTH, C. P., Semantics and pragmatics of the lambda calculus, Ph.D. thesis, Oxford.

[Will82]. WILLIAMS, J. H., Notes on the FP style of functional programming. *Functional Programming and its Applications*, (ed. DARLINGTON et al.), Cambridge University Press, 1982, pp. 73-101.